Turn your eyes upon Jesus

Mark

by Jason Meyer

thegoodbook
COMPANY

Mark For You

These studies are adapted from *Mark For You*. If you are reading *Mark For You* alongside this Good Book Guide, here is how the studies in this booklet link to the chapters of *Mark For You*:

Study One → Ch 1-2   Study Six → Ch 5-6
Study Two → Ch 3   Study Seven → Ch 7-9
Study Three → Ch 4   Study Eight → Ch 10-11
Study Four → Ch 5   Study Nine → Ch 12-13
Study Five → Ch 6   Study Ten → Ch 14

Find out more about *Mark For You* at:
www.thegoodbook.com/for-you

Turn your eyes upon Jesus
The Good Book Guide to Mark
© Jason Meyer/The Good Book Company, 2022
Series Consultants: Tim Chester, Tim Thornborough,
                 Anne Woodcock, Carl Laferton

Published by:
The Good Book Company

thegoodbook.com | thegoodbook.co.uk
thegoodbook.com.au | thegoodbook.co.nz | thegoodbook.co.in

ISBN: 9781784983031

Printed in Turkey

CONTENTS

Introduction: Good Book Guides

Every Bible-study group is different—yours may take place in a church building, in a home or in a cafe, on a train, over a leisurely mid-morning coffee or squashed into a 30-minute lunch break. Your group may include new Christians, mature Christians, non-Christians, moms and tots, students, businessmen or teens. That's why we've designed these *Good Book Guides* to be flexible for use in many different situations.

Our aim in each session is to uncover the meaning of a passage, and see how it fits into the "big picture" of the Bible. But that can never be the end. We also need to appropriately apply what we have discovered to our lives. Let's take a look at what is included:

⊕ **Talkabout:** Most groups need to "break the ice" at the beginning of a session, and here's the question that will do that. It's designed to get people talking around a subject that will be covered in the course of the Bible study.

⊕ **Investigate:** The Bible text for each session is broken up into manageable chunks, with questions that aim to help you understand what the passage is about. The **Leader's Guide** contains **guidance for questions**, and sometimes ⊗ additional "follow-up" questions.

⊙ **Explore more (optional):** These questions will help you connect what you have learned o other parts of the Bible, so you can begin to fit it all together like a jig-saw; or occasionally look at a part of the passage that's not dealt with in detail in the main study.

→ **Apply:** As you go through a Bible study, you'll keep coming across **apply** sections. These are questions to get the group discussing what the Bible teaching means in practice for you and your church. ⊡ **Getting personal** is an opportunity for you to think, plan and pray about the changes that you personally may need to make as a result of what you have learned.

↑ **Pray:** We want to encourage prayer that is rooted in God's word—in line with his concerns, purposes, and promises. So each session ends with an opportunity to review the truths and challenges highlighted by the Bible study, and turn them into prayers of request and thanksgiving.

The **Leader's Guide** and introduction provide historical background information, explanations of the Bible texts for each session, ideas for **optional extra** activities, and guidance on how best to help people uncover the truths of God's word.

Why study Mark?

Church history has not always been kind to the Gospel of Mark. It has sometimes been seen as the least important Gospel simply because it is the shortest. Perhaps I picked up on these negative vibes and allowed them to color my view of Mark's Gospel. I still remember the first time I taught through it. I entered my study of Mark with low expectations and a somewhat impatient eagerness to get to the longer Gospels.

But I was wrong and my life was changed. If I have a first love now in Scripture, it is this Gospel and the Jesus who stands forth from its pages.

Mark's Gospel is fast-paced and action-packed. Mark uses the word "immediately" forty-one times! He does not meander with his message. He narrates this story in such a way that in town after town and story after story the message sounds: *The Son of God has come!*

But in the midst of this consistent message, there is a mystery that keeps building. Conflict and confusion abound because people struggle mightily to see clearly who Jesus is and why he has come. The mystery and the suspense build up a head of steam as the Son gets closer and closer to Calvary. It is only at the cross that someone finally puts the pieces together and confesses that the crucified Christ is the divine Son of God (Mark 15:39).

Mark portrays Jesus in a way that is stunningly compelling. Jesus' unrivaled power and wisdom leave us with a sense of awe, but the portrayal of his unparalleled heart touches us even more deeply. Jesus pours out his love on many different people in story after story all the way to the crescendo of the cross. It was there that God poured out his wrath on him so that he could pour out his love on us through him.

This study guide does not cover every part of Mark's Gospel in detail. Instead it goes through section by section, helping you to see the overall structure of Mark and how the key themes fit together. As you study, let this stunning portrayal of Jesus challenge your perception of him and of yourself. Turn your eyes to Jesus, and be transformed.

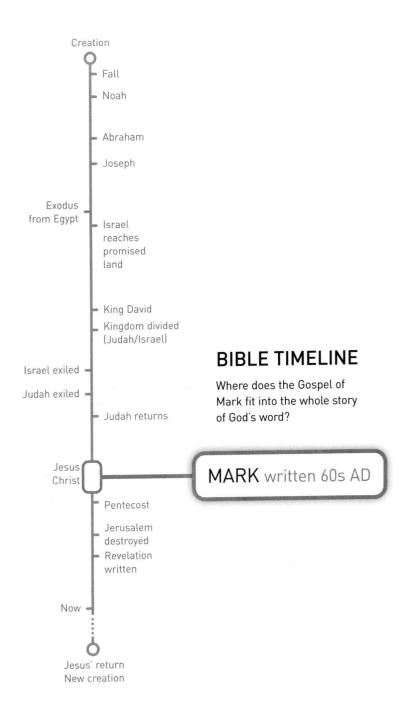

Creation

Fall

Noah

Abraham

Joseph

Exodus from Egypt

Israel reaches promised land

King David

Kingdom divided (Judah/Israel)

Israel exiled

Judah exiled

Judah returns

Jesus Christ

Pentecost

Jerusalem destroyed

Revelation written

Now

Jesus' return New creation

BIBLE TIMELINE

Where does the Gospel of Mark fit into the whole story of God's word?

MARK written 60s AD

1

INTRODUCING THE SON OF GOD

⊕ talkabout

1. What do you know about the Gospel of Mark? What do you hope to get out of it?

⊕ investigate

> ❯ Read Mark 1:1-13

2. Mark gets right to the point. What is his Gospel about (v 1)? What claim is he making about Jesus?

DICTIONARY

Gospel (v 1): good news.
Baptizing (v 4): dunking in water.
Judea (v 5): the region around Jerusalem.
Locust (v 6): a type of insect.
Galilee (v 9): a region north of Judea.

But Mark doesn't want you to just take his word for it.

3. In the promise God made through Isaiah, who would the messenger prepare the way for (v 3)?

• Who is this messenger (v 4)?

optional

⊡ explore more

Mark 1:2-3 is actually a mixed quotation from three places.

❯ Read Exodus 23:20-21; Malachi 3:1; Isaiah 40:3

In Exodus 23, God is delivering his people from Egypt into their own land.

How is the angel in Exodus 23:20 going to help God's people?

In Mark 1:4-5, how is John helping God's people?

It's significant that John baptizes people in the Jordan River (v 5). This was the border between the wilderness and the promised land. It's as if people are entering the promised land all over again.

How does Malachi 3:1 help us understand what it means that John is preparing the way for the Lord?

What detail in Isaiah 40:3 is fulfilled by John?

4. Look at what John says and does (v 4-5). How is this preparing the way for the Lord?

⊡ getting personal

John came to get people ready for Jesus' coming. Taking God seriously meant taking their own sin seriously! Imagine Jesus were coming to visit you. Is there anything you would want to change about your life to get ready for his coming?

5. What does John say about Jesus (v 7-8)?

6. What do we learn about Jesus from what happens next (v 10-11)?

People are being baptized as a sign of their repentance. So what is Jesus doing in that water? He does not need to repent! Jesus is identifying with the need of his people. Humans are not good enough for God. But Jesus came to identify with us, to help us, and to die for us—to bring us to God.

⮕ apply

7. How does this passage call us to respond to Jesus?

⮇ investigate

> ▶ Read Mark 1:14-28

8. What is Jesus' message (v 15)? What does he want people to do?

DICTIONARY

Sea of Galilee (v 16): a large lake.
Capernaum (v 21): a town in Galilee.
Synagogue (v 21): a building where Jews met locally to worship God.

"The kingdom of God is at hand" means that the King has come. God is intervening in human affairs.

9. In the following scenes, how do these people respond to Jesus' words?

• Simon, Andrew, James, and John (v 16-20)

- The unclean spirit in the synagogue (v 23-26)

- The other people in the synagogue (v 22, 27-28)

10. What do the people in the synagogue mean in verse 27 when they say that Jesus has authority?

- How has he demonstrated that authority so far?

What Jesus says, happens. This is another proof of his identity as God—the one who spoke the world into being (Genesis 1).

Jesus next continues to cast out demons and heal diseases (Mark 1:29-34).

11. How do you think casting out demons and healing diseases fit into Jesus' mission statement (v 15)?

In the ancient world, a herald would go ahead of an army and warn people to accept terms of peace. That is what Jesus is doing when he calls people to repent and believe. When we repent, we confess that we have tried to be our own king and we accept Jesus as Lord instead.

➡ apply

12. Based on what you've read in this study, what could you say about Jesus to those who don't yet know him?

⊡ getting personal

Take some time to reflect on your own view of Jesus. Do you believe he is God? Do you recognize his authority and rule in your life? Why, or why not? As you get to know Jesus better in these studies, are you willing to be challenged in your assumptions about him and your response to him?

⬆ pray

Reflect together on the person of Jesus. Pray that the words of the hymn "Be Thou My Vision" would be true of you this week:

"Riches I heed not, nor vain, empty praise.
 Thou mine inheritance, now and always.
 Thou and thou only the first in my heart.
 High King of heaven, my treasure thou art."

(Mary Elizabeth Byrne)

2 Mark 2:1 – 3:6
A MAN OF AUTHORITY

The story so far

Mark's introduction leaves no room for doubt: Jesus is the Son of God, who came to rule over our lives. Repent, believe, and follow him!

⊕ talkabout

1. What do you think people today base their sense of right and wrong on?

⊕ investigate

Today's study features a series of five controversies in which the scribes (religious teachers) repeatedly challenge what Jesus is doing.

> **Read Mark 2:1-17**

2. What's the scene in verses 1-4? Why do the men have to dig through the roof?

DICTIONARY

Paralytic (v 3): someone who is unable to walk.
Blaspheming (v 7): speaking wrongly or disrespectfully about God.
Pharisees (v 16): religious teachers.

3. Why is Jesus' response surprising (v 5)?

• Why do the scribes have a problem with what Jesus has said (v 6-7)?

4. Why does healing the man prove that Jesus has authority to forgive sins (v 8-12)?

5. What does the man have to do in order to be forgiven?

The second controversy also involves sinful people: the tax collectors (v 13-16). Tax collectors were despised. The Jewish system of religion regarded them as hopelessly lost. But Jesus is allowing them to be his followers (v 14, 15)!

6. Why is Jesus eating with the tax collectors (v 17)?

A seismic shift has taken place. God's kingdom is near—and Jesus has the authority to say who is part of it. Those who are part of God's kingdom are not those who think they can cleanse themselves of sin but those who recognize their need for a Savior.

⮕ apply

7. As Jesus' followers, why is it important to keep reminding ourselves of how much we need Jesus?

- As a church, how can we clearly communicate to outsiders both the seriousness of sin and the heart of Jesus to receive sinners?

☺ getting personal

What needs (of any kind) do you have at the moment? Bring them to Jesus in prayer.

⬇ investigate

❯ **Read Mark 2:18 – 3:6**

> ### DICTIONARY
>
> **Fasting (2:18):** not eating.
> **Wineskin (v 22):** a bag made of animal skin, used to store wine.
> **David (v 25):** a king of Israel.
> **The house of God (v 26):** the tabernacle or temple, where God was said to dwell.
> **Bread of the Presence (v 26):** special bread kept in the temple.
> **Herodians (3:6):** a political group supporting King Herod.

8. What is the Pharisees' problem in each of these scenes (2:18, 23-4; 3:2)?

Jesus could criticize the Pharisees' rules (which are manmade traditions, not God's law)—but instead he takes a different tactic.

9. How does Jesus recalibrate the question about fasting (2:19-20)?

10. If the old wineskin and cloth represent the Pharisees' traditions and the new wine and patch are Jesus' teaching, what do these pictures help us understand (v 21-22)?

Jesus gives a similar answer to the Pharisees' next question. "The Son of Man [i.e. Jesus himself] is lord even of the Sabbath" (v 28). Jesus is the fixed point of reference to which every understanding of what is right and wrong must relate.

ⓘ **explore more**

optional

❯ **Re-read Mark 3:1-6**

How does Jesus' question in verse 4 expose where the Pharisees have gone wrong?

Why do you think they remain silent?

What does this story show about Jesus' priorities in deciding what is right and wrong?

11. How do the Pharisees respond to what Jesus has said (v 6)?

• But why is what Jesus has said throughout this study actually incredibly good news?

⊟ apply

12. Think about the traditions, routines, and unwritten rules you have in what you do at church (in services, study groups, youth groups, or other ministries). Is there anything that you are upholding as right or wrong that could actually get in the way of people coming to Jesus? What changes could be made?

⊡ getting personal

What tradition could you start in your own life that would help you to keep acknowledging your need for Jesus and celebrating all that he has done for you?

⊤ pray

Spend time praising Jesus as the one who has authority to forgive sins and to say what is right and wrong. Confess your sins and ask for cleansing. Rejoice at the forgiveness that can be found in him!

3
Mark 3:7 – 4:34
OUTSIDERS AND INSIDERS

The story so far

Mark's introduction leaves no room for doubt: Jesus is the Son of God, who came to rule over our lives. Repent, believe, and follow him!

The religious leaders repeatedly challenge what Jesus is doing. But he is the one with true authority: right and wrong revolve around him.

⊕ talkabout

1. How do you become an "insider" in someone's life? What do you have to do to really get to know them?

⊕ investigate

> **Read Mark 3:7-10, 13-15**

2. What are the differences between the crowds and the apostles in how they relate to Jesus?

DICTIONARY

Idumea (v 8): a region south of Judea.
Tyre and Sidon (v 8): cities to the north of Israel, in modern-day Lebanon.

The rest of chapter 3 shows us more divergent responses to Jesus.

> **Read Mark 3:20-35**

3. What are the teachers of the law accusing Jesus of (v 22)?

• How does Jesus reveal the flaw in their logic (v 23-26)?

4. What must Jesus be doing in order to cast out demons (v 27)?

• And what are the scribes doing when they accuse him of having an evil spirit (v 29-30)?

The irony is that the scribes who accuse Jesus have themselves become aligned with Satan in opposing Jesus. They think he is outside God's kingdom, but it's really they who are outside God's kingdom.

5. Look at the start and end of the passage (v 20-21, 31-35). Where do you think Jesus' family stand—are they inside or outside the kingdom? Why?

➔ apply

6. What would it look like to respond like the following people today?
- The crowds

- The scribes

- Jesus' mother and brothers

- How can we make sure we respond like the apostles instead?

☺ getting personal

Assess your own attitude toward Jesus honestly. Which of the traps outlined in question 6 are you personally most likely to fall into? What habits could you build into your life to help you respond as the disciples do?

⊕ investigate

❯ Read Mark 4:1-20

7. What are the four types of soil, and what responses to Jesus' preaching do these represent (v 2-8, 14-20)?

8. Which "soils" do you think are represented by the various people we saw in Mark 3?

9. Who does Jesus explain the parable to (v 10)?

10. Why does he use parables and not explain them clearly to everyone (v 11-12)?

These verses show that Jesus alone can reveal the secrets of the kingdom. Not everyone can see God's reign at work in what Jesus is doing. He has to disclose it. Only the insiders will understand.

⊡ explore more

> ❯ Read Mark 4:21-34

These four short parables shatter all expectations about the kingdom of God.

The lamp in verses 21-22 is Jesus. What does this parable tell us about how we can find out the secrets of the kingdom?

What does the parable of the measure (v 24-25) call us to do?

What does the parable of the growing seed (v 26-29) tell us about how God's kingdom grows?

What does the parable of the mustard seed (v 30-32) tell us about why Jesus' work seems small or hidden at first?

11. Who are the insiders in God's kingdom, according to what you have read in this study?

⤷ apply

12. In what ways can we hear Jesus' words but not really listen to them? How can we avoid this?

⊞ getting personal

God fixes our broken eyes and ears and hearts; then he calls us to use them. Hebrews 4:7 says, "Today, if you hear his voice, do not harden your hearts." How can you put this into practice this week?

⬆ pray

Pray that God would make you good soil: to give you ears that hear Jesus' words and hearts that obey. Pray that he would make you fruitful.

Then pray for others you know who seem to be the other types of soil. Ask that God would intervene and change their hearts, or keep them following him.

4 Mark 4:35 – 5:43
FEAR AND FAITH

The story so far

Jesus is the Son of God, who came to rule over our lives. The religious leaders' challenges reveal that Jesus is the one with true authority.

He is also the only one who can make someone an insider or an outsider in God's kingdom. Insiders are those who listen to him and do his will.

⊕ talkabout

1. What might make a person seem scary—or not scary at all?

⊕ investigate

▶ Read Mark 4:35 – 5:20

2. In the first story (4:35-41), Jesus asks the disciples why they are afraid. Why shouldn't they be?

DICTIONARY

Stern (4:38): the back of a boat.
Perishing (v 38): dying.
Rebuked (v 39): told off.
Gerasenes (5:1): a non-Jewish people group.
Unclean spirit (v 2): demon.
Shackles (v 4): metal rings used to bind arms or legs.
Adjure (v 7): solemnly beg, urge.
Legion (v 9): army.
Decapolis (v 20): the Gentile region to the east of Galilee.

• But why are they still afraid in verse 41?

The disciples have seen how powerful Jesus is. But the next two stories reveal even more about what Jesus is like.

3. When other people have met the demon-possessed man, what has happened (5:3-4)?

• What's different about his encounter with Jesus (v 6-13)?

This man has an entire army of demons living in him and tormenting him (v 9). But they are no match for the almighty army of One!

⊙ **explore more**

optional

There are two key Old Testament echoes in this story.

The first is from the exodus, when God rescued his people from slavery. The enemy army drowned in the sea (Exodus 14:26-29). Now an army of demons has drowned in the sea.

The second is from Isaiah.

❯ **Read Isaiah 65:1-4**

In Mark 5, Jesus is in the country of the Gerasenes (v 1)—that is, non-Jews. These people thought they had nothing to do with the God of Israel.

What details can you spot in Isaiah 65 that are relevant to this situation?

What is God's attitude to these people (Isaiah 65:1)?

How does Jesus exemplify this attitude?

4. The crowds can see that Jesus is powerful. How do they respond (v 17)?

- Why do you think the formerly demon-possessed man responds differently (v 18)?

⊡ **getting personal**

How eager are you to be with Jesus? How much of your everyday life is he a part of? How could you take advantage of his presence with you in each moment?

5. Jesus wants the man to tell people about his power—and what else (v 19)?

⊕ apply

6. Jesus' mercy calls us to mission. What could you say about "how much the Lord has done for you and how he has had mercy on you" this week—and to whom?

⊕ investigate

❯ Read Mark 5:21-43

7. What do you think Jairus believes about Jesus (v 22-23)?

> **DICTIONARY**
>
> **Discharge of blood (v 25):** probably like a period, but flowing continuously, not just once a month.
> **Physicians (v 26):** doctors.
> **Garment (v 27):** clothing.

• What about the woman in the crowd (v 28)?

This woman is a little like the demon-possessed man. In both cases, people tried to do what they could, but they could not help (v 3-4, 26). But the woman believes that Jesus can do what no one else can do.

8. Why is Jesus' question in verse 30 surprising (v 31)?

• Why do you think he asks it? What's the result (v 33)?

Mark wants us to feel the drama of this moment. Jesus has stopped needlessly to talk to this woman—and now the little girl has died (v 35)!

9. What does the impact seem to have been on Jairus' faith in Jesus?

10. What do you think Jairus would have said about Jesus by the end of the story, and why?

☺ **getting personal**

What do you most need to be reminded of at the moment—Jesus' power, his mercy, or his tender love? What will you ask Jesus to do for you?

11. In 4:41, the disciples were afraid because they saw that Jesus could do what no one else can do. Imagine you had witnessed the events of Mark 5 and were now talking to the disciples. What would you say about Jesus? How would you encourage them to respond with faith instead of fear?

⊡ apply

12. What help does what you have read give us for situations that seem impossible, or for times when we are afraid?

⊡ pray

What seemingly impossible situations do you know of today? Lift them to Jesus in prayer, praising him for his compassion, his mercy, and his almighty power.

5 Mark 7:1-37
CLEAN AND UNCLEAN

The story so far

Jesus is the Son of God, who came to rule over our lives. The religious leaders' challenges reveal that Jesus is the one with true authority.

He is also the only one who can make someone an insider or an outsider in God's kingdom. Insiders are those who listen to him and do his will.

The stories of the storm, the demon-possessed man, Jairus' daughter, and the bleeding woman reveal that Jesus is powerful, merciful, and compassionate.

⊕ talkabout

1. What's the dirtiest you've ever been? What did being dirty stop you from doing?

⊕ investigate

We are in the middle of a long section of signs which reveal Jesus' identity (4:35 – 8:21). There is a rhythm of bread miracles and boat miracles, especially in chapters 6 and 8, which we'll look at in the next study. But for now we'll focus on chapter 7 and the theme of clean and unclean.

▶ Read Mark 7:1-23

DICTIONARY

Elders (v 3): ancestors, or leaders in a community.
Hypocrites (v 6): people who say one thing and do another.
Doctrines (v 7): (here) true teaching from God.
Reviles (v 10): insults.

Corban (v 11): an offering to God.
Void (v 13): empty, meaningless.
Coveting (v 22): wanting what isn't yours.
Deceit (v 22): lying.
Slander (v 22): saying bad things about people.

2. What traditions are Jesus' disciples ignoring (v 1-5)?

This was not just a hygiene issue. It was a question of ritual purity. People believed that if you did not wash hands, cups, and vessels before eating, you would be "unclean" before God—unworthy to enter his presence. The Pharisees are basically saying that Jesus doesn't care about the holiness of God. They think that his standards are much lower than God's standards.

3. How does Jesus assess the Pharisees' traditions (v 6-8)?

4. What is more important than external rituals or words (v 6)?

5. What can make a person unclean, in fact (v 15, 20-23)?

getting personal

Jesus wants us to be uncompromising about holiness. Look at verses 21-22 again and reflect on your own heart. Where do you need God's forgiveness and help to change?

⊖ apply

6. In what ways can we fall into the trap of honoring God externally while being far from him internally? How could we avoid this?

⊕ investigate

❯ **Read Mark 7:24-30**

DICTIONARY

Tyre and Sidon (v 24): cities in modern-day Lebanon. **Syrophoenician (v 26):** someone from what is now Lebanon and western Syria.

7. What do you think the Pharisees would have thought of the Syrophoenician woman (v 25-26)? Would they have wanted Jesus to go near her?

8. How does Jesus acknowledge the difference between Jews and Gentiles (v 27)?

Jesus' response to the woman in verse 27 seems offensive at first glance. But this is not an insult. Jesus uses a form of the word for dogs which means "puppies." It is a term of affection.

9. What are the woman's expectations about how Jesus will treat Gentiles (v 28)?

There is an order to Jesus' mission. He came first of all to show Israel that he is the fulfillment of all that God promised to them. Later, he would send out his disciples to all the nations. The Pharisees regarded Gentiles as totally unclean, but Jesus welcomed them. Many Jews would reject Jesus, but many Gentiles would become children in Jesus' kingdom.

10. What is it that makes the woman clean?

11. What happens to the woman's daughter and why (v 30)?

⊡ explore more

optional

Jesus now takes a long journey, staying in Gentile territory.

❯ Read Mark 7:31-37

Why does Jesus touch the man's ears and tongue? He can just say the word and the man will be healed! The glorious, wonderful answer is that Jesus is using sign language. He is explaining using touch what he is going to do.

What does that tell us about Jesus' attitude toward the man?

What do people conclude about Jesus (v 37)?

Jesus changes everything. The Pharisees want to decide who and what is clean or unclean. But Jesus takes what is unclean and makes it clean. Wherever he goes, he makes things new!

⊖ apply

12. Based on everything you've read in the study, what should we do when we have sinned?

⊡ getting personal

Where do you long for transformation in your life? In what ways do you wish to be made new? Spend some time in prayer, asking for Jesus' help.

⬆ pray

Spend time worshiping Jesus for all he is and all he has done. Ask him to give you clean hearts that truly love and know him, and therefore desire to obey him.

6 HARD HEARTS

The story so far

Jesus is the Son of God, who came to rule over our lives. He is the one with true authority and the only one who can make us insiders in God's kingdom.

The stories of the storm, the demon-possessed man, Jairus' daughter, and the bleeding woman reveal that Jesus is powerful, merciful, and compassionate.

The Pharisees accuse Jesus' followers of being unclean, but Jesus turns the tables on what it really means to be clean or unclean.

⊕ talkabout

1. How forgetful are you? When does forgetfulness not really matter? When does it?

⊥ investigate

This section of Mark has a rhythm of boat miracles (4:35-41; 6:45-51) and bread miracles (6:30-44; 8:1-10)—culminating with bread in the boat (8:11-21)! This cycle reveals more about Jesus' identity and challenges us about our response to him.

The twelve apostles have been sent out to teach about Jesus, cast out demons, and heal the sick (see 6:7-13). We pick up the story as they return.

> **Read Mark 6:30-52**

> **DICTIONARY**
>
> **Apostles (v 30):** the twelve sent out by Jesus in 6:7-13.
> **Desolate (v 31):** deserted.
> **Denarii (v 37):** coins. A denarius was a day's wage for a laborer.
> **The fourth watch of the night (v 48):** 3am to 6am.

2. What does Jesus think and feel about the crowds (v 34)?

This is a big biblical echo. It tells us to look back to Moses, who asked God to appoint a successor for him so that the people would not be "like sheep without a shepherd" (Numbers 27:17). Jesus is that successor!

3. In Mark 6:30-52, how is Jesus like a shepherd?

4. Look at Exodus 16:1-4, 13-16. This is another part of Moses' story. What links can you spot with the feeding of the 5,000?

5. The scene changes in verses 45-48. Where are the disciples and where is Jesus now?

The phrase "pass by them" is another biblical echo. This is exactly what God did for both Moses and Elijah: he passed by them so they could see his glory (Exodus 33:19; 1 Kings 19:11). He was revealing his identity.

"It is I," says Jesus (Mark 6:50). In the original language this is the same phrase that God used to declare his name to Moses: "I AM" (Exodus 34:5-7—it's translated here "the LORD").

6. Why do you think Jesus is repeating these moments from the Old Testament?

• What don't the disciples understand? Why not?

➔ apply

7. Today Jesus reveals to us by his word and through his Spirit. What would it look like to read the Bible with a hard heart, even as a believer? What attitude should we have instead?

⊡ getting personal

Why might fear be the response of a hard heart? What difference has it made to fearful situations in the past when you have reminded yourself of who Jesus is? What could you do to help others who are facing fearful situations to "take heart" (v 50)?

⬇ investigate

❱ Read Mark 8:1-21

8. What does the situation in 8:1-4 have in common with the one in 6:30-38?

The disciples' memory should kick in at this point. They have been here before. They should expect Jesus to perform a similar miracle. Disappointingly, though, they respond the same way as last time (8:4).

The rest of the story (v 5-10) follows the same pattern. All the people eat and are satisfied, and the disciples pick up the leftovers.

9. Look at verses 11-13. Why do you think Jesus sighs at the Pharisees?

10. If "the leaven of the Pharisees" means responding to Jesus like the Pharisees do, what is Jesus warning the disciples against?

11. How does their response show that they are already falling into that trap (v 16-21)?

⊙ **explore more**

optional

Back in Mark 6, the story of Herod's dealings with John the Baptist reveals what "the leaven of Herod" might be.

❯ Read Mark 6:18-29

What did Herod think about John (v 20)?

What did he do to him in the end (v 27-28)?

What got in the way of his fragile belief (v 21-26)?

❯ Read Mark 6:14-16

Why is Herod's response to Jesus better than the Pharisees'? And in another sense, why is it just as bad?

So what do you think "the leaven of Herod" is?

⊡ **getting personal**

It's easy to look at the disciples and feel smug. How could they keep forgetting the things that Jesus has done? But the question comes right back at us. We've all seen Jesus do things, too. But when the next hard thing comes, we easily forget it all.

What reminders can you set up for yourself of Jesus' identity? How can that help you to handle difficult times well when they come?

⊖ **apply**

12. In what ways can we, even as believers, end up acting as if we've forgotten who Jesus is?

• What should we pray for our hearts?

⬆ pray

Use the words of Psalm 23 and Exodus 34:6-7 to help you celebrate Jesus, the compassionate Shepherd who reveals himself to us and provides for us. Then spend time reflecting and praying that God would remove any hardness in your hearts.

7 Mark 8:22 – 10:52
TRUE GREATNESS

The story so far

Jesus is the Son of God, who came to rule over our lives. He is the one with true authority and the only one who can make us insiders in God's kingdom.

Jesus is powerful, merciful, and compassionate. He turns the tables on what it really means to be clean or unclean and he welcomes sinners.

Jesus' bread and boat miracles reveal who he is. Yet the disciples respond with hard and forgetful hearts.

⊕ talkabout

1. What big desires or hopes do you have for your future? Why?

⊌ investigate

We have come to the turn in the Gospel of Mark. The next section (8:22 – 10:52), which follows Jesus and his disciples as they journey to Jerusalem, begins and ends with the healing of a blind man. These bookends are about physical blindness, but the stories in the middle are about spiritual blindness. This journey to Jerusalem is actually a struggle for sight.

❯ Read Mark 8:22-38

> **DICTIONARY**
>
> **Bethsaida (v 22):** a town near the Sea of Galilee.
> **Caesarea Philippi (v 27):** a town 40 miles north of the Sea of Galilee.
> **Elijah (v 28):** an important figure in the Old Testament (1 Kings 17 – 21; 2 Kings 1 – 2).
>
> **The Christ (v 29):** God's promised King.
> **The Son of Man (v 31):** God's promised King.
> **Rebuke (v 32):** tell off.
> **Satan (v 33):** the devil.
> **Forfeit (v 36):** lose.

2. What is strange about the healing of the blind man (v 22-25)?

This healing is a parable, an object lesson. The blind man represents the disciples. Their spiritual sight is only partial—as we see in the next scene.

3. What does Peter see clearly about Jesus (v 27-29)?

4. What does he rebuke Jesus for and why (v 31-33)?

5. How should seeing the truth about Jesus affect his followers' lives (v 34)?

• Why? What is the warning and what is the promise in this text (v 35-38)?

⊡ getting personal

In this passage Peter learns that we have to let go of worldly thinking in order to embrace the things of God. How does this apply to your life? What good things do you desire? Are you willing to surrender them for Jesus' sake?

⊡ explore more

optional

The next scene gives us a sneak peek at the glorious future mentioned in verse 38.

▶ Read Mark 9:1-13

What are Peter, James, and John seeing (v 1)?

What do they literally see (v 2-4)?

Why does Peter need to hear the statement and the command in verse 7?

But what do the disciples fail to understand (v 9-10)?

⊙ apply

6. What could it look like for us to deny ourselves for Jesus' sake today?

⊙ investigate

▶ Read Mark 9:30-37 and 10:32-52

> **DICTIONARY**
>
> **Gentiles (10:33):** non-Jews.
> **Jericho (v 46):** a town near the Jordan River, north of Jerusalem.

7.   What does Jesus keep on saying about himself (9:30-31; 10:33-34)?

8.   What are the disciples more concerned about (9:34; 10:37)?

9.   What makes someone great, according to 9:35-37?

   • What example of this does Jesus give, and what motive does he provide?

10.   What two different standards of greatness does Jesus describe in 10:42-45?

⊖ apply

11. Who are you "greater" than, according to the world's standards? What can you do to serve them?

12. Think back to the ambitions and hopes you discussed at the start of the study. How does what you've seen in this study change your perspective or priorities?

This section of Mark closes with another story about a blind man. Bartimaeus recognises who Jesus is (v 47) and his request for sight is granted (v 51-52). This man sees Jesus rightly and responds rightly: he follows Jesus on the road toward the cross.

⊡ getting personal

Are you willing to follow Jesus, even when that means suffering and self-denial? Are you convinced that it's worth it? Spend some time reflecting on his words in this study. Be honest about your hesitations and fears and ask for Jesus' help in committing yourself to him.

⊙ pray

Pray for Jesus' help in seeing him, and yourselves, clearly. Commit yourselves afresh to following him.

8

Mark 11:11 – 12:44

JESUS IN THE TEMPLE

The story so far

Jesus is the powerful, merciful, compassionate Son of God. He alone can make us clean and welcome us into God's kingdom.

Jesus' bread and boat miracles reveal who he is. Yet the disciples respond with hard and forgetful hearts.

On the journey to Jerusalem, the disciples fail to see Jesus clearly—recognizing that he is the Messiah yet not understanding the fact that he must suffer.

⊕ talkabout

1. How do you tell if someone really loves God?

⊕ investigate

> **Read Mark 11:11-25**

Jesus' curse on the fig tree (v 14) is not a case of childish anger. Jesus is acting out a parable based on Jeremiah 8:13. Jeremiah described the people as being like a fig tree with no figs: they had not grown or borne fruit but had rejected what God gave them. They were therefore bound for judgment.

The fig tree scene should influence the way we read the next story.

DICTIONARY

Bethany (v 11): a village close to Jerusalem.
Rabbi (v 21): a Jewish teacher.
This mountain (v 23): Jesus is probably looking at Mount Zion, where the temple was built.
Trespasses (v 25): sins.

2. Look at verse 17. Why has God given the people the temple?

• What have they made it into instead?

3. So what does Jesus do (v 15-16)?

The money-changers were there to receive the temple tax which funded the daily sacrifices. The pigeons were being sold as sacrifices. So Jesus is stopping the temple from functioning.

The phrase "den of robbers" helps us understand why.

> **Read Jeremiah 7:9-11**

People in Jeremiah's day believed that coming into the temple would keep them safe from God's judgment—so they could keep sinning. They were like robbers hiding in a cave.

4. What's wrong with this? What do you think they should have been doing instead?

DICTIONARY

Baal (v 9): a false god.
This house (v 10): the temple.
Delivered (v 10): saved.
Abominations (v 10): sins.
Behold (v 11): look.

In Jesus' day, too, the temple is supposed to be a place where people come to God for forgiveness. But once again people are going through the motions without really pursuing God. This is why Jesus puts a stop to the sacrifices.

5. What kind of heart does Jesus want his people to have (v 22-25)?

• Why is forgiving others so important (v 25)?

⊡ **apply**

6. What does this passage teach us about prayer? How can we honor God properly in the way we pray?

⬇ investigate

Mark 11:27 – 12:44 describes Jesus' third trip to the temple and a series of disputes with the religious teachers there.

⊡ explore more

optional

❯ Read Mark 11:27-33

What do the religious leaders ask Jesus first (v 27)? What do you think is their motivation for asking it?

What counter-question does Jesus ask (v 30)? Why is this a trap (v 31-32)?

John's baptism is significant here for two reasons. First, John baptized Jesus—and it was at that baptism that God the Father declared that Jesus is the Son (1:9-11). So it reminds us where Jesus gets his authority. Second, John was sent by God with a baptism of repentance for the forgiveness of sins. It did not involve the temple and the sacrifices. It was free. The only requirement was a repentant heart. So, by mentioning John, Jesus is once again challenging the Jewish religious system.

❯ Read Mark 12:28-44

7. In verses 28-31, what question does the scribe ask and how does Jesus answer it?

> **DICTIONARY**
>
> **Disputing (v 28):** arguing, debating.
> **Israel (v 29):** God's people in the Old Testament.
> **Burnt offering (v 33):** a type of animal sacrifice.
> **Throng (v 37):** crowd.
> **Treasury (v 41):** place where money is kept.
> **Abundance (v 44):** plenty.

8. Why do you think obeying these commandments is better than making sacrifices (v 32-34)?

9. Why will the scribes Jesus talks about in verses 38-40 be condemned?

10. Jesus previously stopped offerings from being made in the temple. So why does he approve of the widow's offering (v 41-44)?

⤷ apply

11. Think about some sacrifices people might make for the Lord today. How can these be an expression of faith?

• But when do they become just formalities?

☺ getting personal

What sacrifices do you make for God? What do you think your motivation is?

12. How can we guard our hearts against hypocrisy and truly devote ourselves to God?

⬆ **pray**

Praise God for all that he is—the only one worthy of our total devotion.

Then spend time praying for particular neighbors you could love and serve this week.

9 Mark 13:28 – 14:72
THE END DRAWS NEAR

The story so far

Jesus is the powerful, merciful, compassionate Son of God. He alone can make us clean and welcome us into God's kingdom.

On the journey to Jerusalem, the disciples fail to see Jesus clearly—recognizing that he is the Messiah yet not understanding the fact that he must suffer.

Jesus challenges the temple system in Jerusalem, revealing the hypocrisy of the Pharisees and commending the true devotion shown by a poor woman.

⊕ talkabout

1. When you're about to see a loved one you haven't seen for a long time, what might you do to get ready?

⊕ investigate

As Jesus' time in the temple comes to an end, he predicts its destruction (13:2). Then he continues to speak about the future (v 3-27). He seems to be talking about two timeframes at once: the destruction of the temple in AD 70, and the end of the age, when Jesus will come again.

❯ Read Mark 13:28-37

2. Why have the disciples got to "stay awake" (v 32-37)? What does Jesus mean by this?

• What time periods does he mention (v 35)?

We can read this part of the chapter as being about the second coming, just like earlier sections. But Mark 13 is not only about the second coming. Jesus is also talking about events that are just about to take place. The Lord is coming now!

❯ Read Mark 14:10-31

It's evening (v 17)—one of the times Jesus told his disciples to watch out for.

3. What moments in this passage show us that Jesus is in control of what is happening?

• Why is that important?

⊡ getting personal

This text heralds the rock-solid truth that God rules and reigns over this world in meticulous detail. He is not just generally in control over some things or many things or most things, but meticulously in control of all things.

How does this help you in your life this week? Or who do you know who needs to hear this truth?

4. What do verses 22-25 reveal about why Jesus came?

Then it's midnight (v 26)—signaled by the singing of a hymn, part of the Passover traditions.

5. How do Peter and the other disciples demonstrate their lack of "alertness" in verses 27-31? How would you describe their response?

→ **apply**

6. Jesus' command to stay awake is for all of us (13:37). Now it is Jesus' second coming that we need to be ready for. We need to be spiritually awake. What do you think it looks like to be ready for Jesus' return? Look at the following verses to help you.

• 13:34

• 13:21-23 (if you have time)

• 14:27-31

• 14:37-38 (if you have time)

⊕ investigate

❯ Read Mark 14:32-42

7. How does Mark help us feel the agony of Jesus in these verses?

8. How does he emphasize the failure of the disciples to stay awake?

⊡ getting personal

Have you ever literally fallen asleep while trying to pray? What can you do practically to develop a regular prayer slot, in which you don't fall asleep?! How might Jesus' example in Gethsemane inspire and help you with your own prayer life?

❯ Read Mark 14:53-72

9. What moments in Jesus' trial (v 53-65) hint at who he really is?

• Yet how do we see the total rejection of Jesus as Lord here?

10. What do Jesus' responses in verses 60-62 tell us about him?

⊡ explore more

Jesus' words in verse 62 refer to a prophecy about the Messiah in Daniel 7.

> **Read Daniel 7:13-14**

What is given to the Son of Man?

What is his future?

How might this change the way we look at our own future?

11. Why does Peter deny Jesus (14:66-72)? What do you think is going through his mind throughout this scene?

The rooster crows (v 72)—the third moment in time that Jesus highlighted in 13:35. Peter has failed to be alert and awake. But there is one more time period left: morning. This will come in 15:1, as Jesus is delivered over to be crucified. This is the moment Jesus came for: the moment when he will most truly be revealed.

⮕ apply

12. We have all failed Jesus, denied him, and rejected him at different times. But why does Mark 14 offer us hope?

⬆ pray

Confess your sins and failings to Jesus. Praise him for his willingness to endure such agony for you. Ask for help in living for him, in readiness for his return.

0 Mark 15:16 – 16:8
THE DIVINE KING

The story so far

Jesus is the powerful, merciful, compassionate Son of God. Yet the disciples fail to see him clearly—they don't understand the fact that he must suffer.

Jesus challenges the temple system in Jerusalem, revealing the hypocrisy of the Pharisees and commending the true devotion shown by a poor woman.

In the run-up to the cross, we see how Jesus is in complete control, yet also in deep agony. He warns the disciples to be awake to who he is, but they fail.

⊕ talkabout

1. Why do you think it can hurt so much to be rejected or abandoned by others?

⊕ investigate

▶ Read Mark 15:16-39

2. How does the soldiers' mockery of Jesus actually reveal who he really is (v 16-20)?

> ### DICTIONARY
> **Battalion (v 16):** about 600 soldiers.
> **Reed (v 19):** a symbol of kingship.
> **Homage (v 19):** special honor or respect.
> **Cyrene (v 21):** a city in modern-day Libya.
> **Myrrh (v 23):** a drug used as a painkiller.
> **Casting lots (v 24):** like rolling dice.
> **The third, sixth, ninth hour (v 25, 33):** 9am, 12 noon, 3pm.
> **Inscription (v 26):** writing.
> **Derided (v 29):** mocked.
> **Reviled (v 32):** insulted.
> **Forsaken (v 34):** abandoned, rejected.
> **Centurion (v 39):** a Roman army official.

3. In verses 21-27, what do we find out about how Jesus is treated?

4. Who else is Jesus rejected and mocked by (v 29-32)?

- Jesus is King. If that's so, what should he do, according to these mockers?

5. Where does the climax of Jesus' suffering and rejection by others come?

In this climactic moment, the Father placed the sin of the world upon his Son. Jesus drank the cup of condemnation to the dregs—experiencing the searing pain of separation from God and the damnation of God.

"Why have you forsaken me?" The answer is: so that sinners could be accepted. Jesus was forsaken so that those who are in him would never be.

6. What happened as Jesus breathed his last (v 37-39)?

The temple curtain separated off the Most Holy Place, which represented God's presence. No one but the high priest was able to enter behind the curtain. Now it is torn in two. Access to God is available.

• What do you think made the centurion realize who Jesus was?

☺ getting personal

The cross can sometimes become like a painting hung on a wall. We believe it, but it blends into the background. Take the opportunity now to really gaze at the cross. Imagine you were there. What strikes you or moves you?

Jesus' cry in verse 34 comes from Psalm 22. This psalm opens with the question of why God has forsaken the Messiah. But it ends with the answer: so that the nations can come to God in worship.

❯ **Read Psalm 22:29-31**

⮕ apply

7. How does it feel to know that Jesus was forsaken by his Father so that you could be accepted?

• What are some ways in which you can put into practice Psalm 22's call to worship Jesus, serve him, and proclaim that "he has done it"?

⊡ explore more

The evening of Jesus' burial is full of surprises.

❯ Read Mark 15:40-47

Why is Joseph of Arimathea a surprising disciple of Jesus (v 43)?

Why is Pilate surprised (v 44)?

Jesus died as a convicted criminal, but how is he buried?

⊡ investigate

❯ Read Mark 16:1-8

> **DICTIONARY**
>
> **Anoint (v 1):** apply ointment or oil.

8. What are the women expecting when they go to the tomb (16:1-3)?

9. What do they discover instead (v 4-6)?

10. Why do you think they are so afraid (v 8)?

11. The Gospel of Mark ends very abruptly. How does that affect our final impression of Jesus?

Are you ever discouraged by all the ways that people mock, slander, and slight the worth of Jesus today? In the midst of that mockery, what hope does this text give you personally?

⇥ **apply**

12. In what ways does the resurrection of Jesus change our perspective on life here and now?

• What will you do and say in response?

⬆ **pray**

As we close our study of this portrait of Jesus, what has struck you the most about who he is and what he is like? What fresh resolve do you have for how to worship and serve him in the future? Spend time praising him and praying for one another.

Turn your eyes upon Jesus

Mark

LEADER'S GUIDE

Leader's Guide

INTRODUCTION

Leading a Bible study can be a bit like herding cats—everyone has a different idea of what the passage could be about, and a different line of enquiry that they want to pursue. But a good group leader is more than someone who just referees this kind of discussion. You will want to:

- correctly understand and handle the Bible passage. But also…

- encourage and train the people in your group to do this for themselves. Don't fall into the trap of spoon-feeding people by simply passing on the information in the Leader's Guide. Then…

- make sure that no Bible study is finished without everyone knowing how the passage is relevant for them. What changes do you all need to make in the light of the things you have been learning? And finally…

- encourage the group to turn all that has been learned and discussed into prayer.

Your Bible-study group is unique, and you are likely to know better than anyone the capabilities, backgrounds, and circumstances of the people you are leading. That's why we've designed these guides with a number of optional features. If they're a quiet bunch, you might want to spend longer on *talkabout*. If your time is limited, you can choose to skip *explore more*, or get people to look at these questions at home. Can't get enough of Bible study? Well, some studies have optional extra homework projects. As leader, you can adapt and select the material to the needs of your particular group.

So what's in the Leader's Guide?
The main thing that this Leader's Guide will help you to do is to understand the major teaching points in the passage you are studying, and how to apply them. As well as guidance for the questions, the Leader's Guide for each session contains the following important sections:

THE BIG IDEA

One or two key sentences will give you the main point of the session. This is what you should be aiming to have fixed in people's minds as they leave the Bible study. And it's the point you need to head back toward when the discussion goes off at a tangent.

SUMMARY

An overview of the passage, including plenty of useful historical background information.

OPTIONAL EXTRA

Usually this is an introductory activity that ties in with the main theme of the Bible study, and is designed to "break the ice" at the beginning of a session. Or it may be a "homework project" that people can tackle during the week.

So let's take a look at the various different features of a Good Book Guide:

⊕ talkabout

Each session kicks off with a discussion question, based on the group's opinions or experiences. It's designed to get people talking and thinking in a general way about the main subject of the Bible study.

⊕ investigate

The first thing you and your group need to know is what the Bible passage is about, which is the purpose of these questions. But watch out—people may come up with answers based on their experiences or teaching they have heard in the past, without referring to the passage at all. It's amazing how often we can get through a Bible study without actually looking at the Bible! If you're stuck for an answer, the Leader's Guide contains guidance for questions. These are the answers to direct your group to. This information isn't meant to be read out to people—ideally, you want them to discover these answers from the Bible for themselves. Sometimes there are optional follow-up questions (see ⊗ in guidance for questions) to help you help your group get to the answer.

⊡ explore more

These questions generally point people to other relevant parts of the Bible. They are useful for helping your group to see how the passage fits into the "big picture" of the whole Bible. These sections are OPTIONAL—only use them if you have time. Remember that it's better to finish in good time having really grasped one big thing from the passage, than to try and cram everything in.

⊖ apply

We want to encourage you to spend more time working at application—too often, it is simply tacked on at the end. In the Good Book Guides, apply sections are mixed in with the investigate sections of the study. We hope that people will realize that application is not just an optional extra, but rather, the whole purpose of studying the

Bible. We do Bible study so that our lives can be changed by what we hear from God's word. If you skip the application, the Bible study hasn't achieved its purpose.

These questions draw out practical lessons that we can all learn from the Bible passage. You can review what has been learned so far, and think about practical differences that this should make in our churches and our lives. The group gets the opportunity to talk about what they personally have learned.

⊡ getting personal

These can be done at home, but it is well worth allowing a few moments of quiet reflection during the study for each person to think and pray about specific changes they need to make in their own lives. Why not have a time for reporting back at the beginning of the following session, so that everyone can be encouraged and challenged by one another to make application a priority?

⊕ pray

In Acts 4:25-30 the first Christians quoted Psalm 2 as they prayed in response to the persecution of the apostles by the Jewish religious leaders. Today however, it's not as common for Christians to base prayers on the truths of God's word as it once was. As a result, our prayers tend to be weak, superficial, and self-centered rather than bold, visionary, and God-centered.

The prayer section is based on what has been learned from the Bible passage. How different our prayer times would be if we were genuinely responding to what God has said to us through his word.

1

Mark 1:1-45
INTRODUCING THE SON OF GOD

THE BIG IDEA
Jesus is the Son of God, who came to rule over our lives. Repent, believe, and follow him.

SUMMARY
Mark gets right to the point. His introduction consists of four testimonies that Jesus is the divine Son of God. He starts by stating that his Gospel is about "Jesus Christ, the Son of God" (v 1). But he doesn't want us to just take his word for it. He next shows how God has spoken through the prophets in a way that accords with his own testimony (v 2-3). He uses a mixed quotation from Exodus 23:20; Malachi 3:1; and Isaiah 40:3. These texts highlight the fact that the Lord had promised to come, and show the careful preparation that must precede his coming.

Third, Mark gives us the testimony of John the Baptist (Mark 1:4-8). John is the messenger promised by the prophets. He prepares people to receive Jesus by a baptism of repentance. This highlights the true problem (people's sin against God) and the solution (repentance). John promises that someone is coming who is mightier than himself and who will baptize people with the Holy Spirit. This could only be God.

Fourth, we have the testimony of God himself (v 9-11). Jesus is baptized—not in order to repent, but in order to identify himself with his people. The heavens are torn open, the Holy Spirit descends, and the voice of God is heard proclaiming Jesus' identity.

Mark's introduction closes with Jesus being driven into the wilderness, where he faces temptation from Satan (v 12-13).

Next we begin the first of the three main movements in Mark: Jesus' ministry in and around Galilee. 1:14-45 is a snapshot of Jesus' ministry. Verses 14-15 outline Jesus' message. He brings the good news that God himself has come to rule, and calls people to repent and believe this good news.

We then witness several demonstrations of Jesus' authority as God's Son. First are two calling narratives (v 16-20). Jesus calls two sets of brothers to follow him, and they immediately do. Next comes a scene in the synagogue in Capernaum (v 21-28). There is a man there who is being controlled by an unclean spirit. The unclean spirit identifies Jesus as a way of confronting him (v 23-24), but Jesus simply commands it to come out of the man, and it does. The onlookers are amazed. Jesus doesn't just speak authoritatively (v 22) but has the authority to make things happen when he speaks (v 27).

Jesus next continues to cast out demons and heal diseases (v 29-34, 40-45). These passages are structured in such a way to show the priority of preaching over healing. Jesus has come as herald of God's kingdom. Healing diseases and casting out demons are signs of the kingdom, confirming his message. When the disciples want Jesus to return to his healing ministry, he declares that they are taking him off mission (v 35-39). Above all, he has come to preach the gospel.

OPTIONAL EXTRA

Play the game Two Truths and a Lie. Each person has to make three claims about themselves. Two must be true, and one is a lie. Everyone else has to guess which is the lie.

GUIDANCE FOR QUESTIONS

1. What do you know about the Gospel of Mark? What do you hope to get out of it? Groups may have many different answers! This is a chance to warm everyone up and encourage them to share their thoughts and feelings as you begin.

2. Mark gets right to the point. What is his Gospel about (v 1)? What claim is he making about Jesus? Jesus is the Son of God. He is the embodiment of the gospel or "good news." He is the eternal God, who has come in the flesh as the promised Messiah (or "Christ").

3. In the promise God made through Isaiah, who would the messenger prepare the way for (v 3)? The Lord. That is, God himself.

• Who is this messenger (v 4)? John.

EXPLORE MORE
Read Exodus 23:20-21; Malachi 3:1; Isaiah 40:3
How is the angel in Exodus 23:20 going to help God's people? The angel will guard their way and tell them what to do.
In Mark 1:4-5, how is John helping God's people? He is preparing them for the arrival of the Lord. He highlights their true problem (sin) and the right solution (repentance). Like the angel in Exodus 23, he is guiding them in what is the right thing to do.
How does Malachi 3:1 help us understand what it means that John is

preparing the way for the Lord? God is going to "suddenly come." A covenant (a binding agreement between God and his people) is going to be made. This points to the new covenant which Jesus brought.
What detail in Isaiah 40:3 is fulfilled by John? John appears "in the wilderness" (Mark 1:4).

4. Look at what John says and does (v 4-5). How is this preparing the way for the Lord? John prepares people to receive the Messiah by a baptism of repentance. This method of preparation highlights the people's true problem (their sin against God) and gives them the solution (repentance).

5. What does John say about Jesus (v 7-8)? John says that Jesus is mighty (see Isaiah 40:10). He says that he himself is not even worthy to do the most menial task for Jesus. He then highlights how much greater the Messiah is by contrasting himself with him. The distinguishing mark of John's ministry is his connection to water. The defining mark of the Messiah's ministry will be his connection to the Holy Spirit. What a contrast! No one can bestow the Spirit in the Old Testament except God. The implication is that the Messiah must be God incarnate.

6. What do we learn about Jesus from what happens next (v 10-11)?
• Jesus comes from Nazareth—an obscure, lowly place (see Nathanael's quip in John 1:46).
• The heavens are torn open in a fulfilment of Isaiah 64:1. It's a sign that God himself is coming down. The barriers between humanity and God are being broken apart.
• The Holy Spirit descends upon Jesus. This gentle hovering presence is similar to the

hovering of the Spirit over the waters at the beginning of creation (Genesis 1:1). It's a sign of the new creation which would be brought through Jesus.

- The Father's voice testifies that Jesus is his "beloved Son." Jesus is the divine Son; not only this, but he is part of a loving relationship with the Father and the Spirit. The Father is pleased with him. This is a reference to Isaiah 42:1, which promises a Servant who will bring justice. So this is a hint about Jesus' mission.

7. APPLY: How does this passage call us to respond to Jesus?
- Believe. The author, the prophets, John the Baptist, and God the Father all testify to Jesus' true identity. They call us to believe that he is the divine Son, come into the world.
- Repent. We have walked in ignorance of and rebellion against God. Coming face-to-face with the arrival of Jesus in the world is an opportunity to confess our sins, repent, and receive forgiveness.

8. What is Jesus' message (v 15)? What does he want people to do? Jesus' claim that "the time is fulfilled" (v 15) highlights the fact that his preaching fulfills Isaiah's prophecies. God's reign has come (see Isaiah 52:7). Jesus is the herald of God's kingdom. He calls people to prepare for the kingdom by repenting and believing the good news of God's coming.

9. In the following scenes, how do these people respond to Jesus' words?
- **Simon, Andrew, James, and John (v 16-20):** They follow him immediately.
- **The unclean spirit in the synagogue (v 23-26):** First it confronts Jesus (v 23-24). Recognizing that the Satanic realm is

under attack, it identifies who Jesus is in a hostile but feeble attempt to confront him. But Jesus simply tells the spirit to be silent and gives it a command to come out of the man. The demon is powerless before the command of the Creator. He convulses the man, lets out a loud chilling demonic shriek, and then does exactly what Jesus commanded.

- **The other people in the synagogue (v 22, 27-28):** They are astonished at his teaching (v 22). Traditionally, scribes taught by quoting other rabbis. But Jesus comes with a direct authority of his own. After he casts out the unclean spirit, they are amazed again (v 27).

10. What do the people in the synagogue mean in verse 27 when they say that Jesus has authority? Jesus doesn't just sound authoritative. He actually has the authority to command. What he says, happens.

- **How has he demonstrated that authority so far?**
  - In the calling narratives (v 16-20). Jesus commands the disciples to follow him, and they immediately do.
  - In his teaching (v 21).
  - In casting out the unclean spirit (v 27).

11. How do you think casting out demons and healing diseases fit into Jesus' mission statement (v 15)? Jesus' main purpose is to preach the good news that the King has come. Healing diseases and casting out demons are signs of the kingdom, confirming his message. Notice that although the crowds are amazed at and attracted by Jesus' miracles, this falls short of true faith. They need to hear his message and repent.

- **Look at verses 35-38. What light do these verses shed on this question?** The disciples want Jesus to return to his healing ministry, but Jesus' statement in verse 38 makes it clear that his priority is to preach.

12. APPLY: Based on what you've read in this study, what could you say about

Jesus to those who don't yet know him? Jesus is the Son of God (v 1, 11), who baptizes people with the Holy Spirit (v 8: i.e. he allows people to come to God). He was promised long before he came (v 2). He is the Lord himself, the King of the world (v 3, 15). He speaks with authority and is powerful to defeat evil and heal diseases (v 21-34). He calls us to repent and promises forgiveness (v 4, 15). He calls us to follow him (v 16-20).

2 Mark 2:1 – 3:6
A MAN OF AUTHORITY

THE BIG IDEA
Jesus has the last word on what is sinful and what is not. He also has authority to forgive. Recognize your need for him and live according to what he says.

SUMMARY
Today's study features a series of five controversies in which the scribes (religious teachers) repeatedly challenge what Jesus is doing. First, Jesus heals a paralytic (2:1-12). Jesus is preaching the word in Capernaum, and four men dig through the roof to get their paralyzed friend into the crowded building. Jesus sees the men's faith and declares that the man's sins are forgiven. The scribes think that this is blasphemy— Jesus is making himself out to be God. So Jesus proves that he has authority to forgive sins by healing the man's paralysis.

The second controversy (v 13-17) involves tax collectors. The Jewish system of religion regarded these men as hopelessly lost. But Jesus is allowing them to be his followers!

Once again the scribes criticize Jesus. But Jesus turns the scribes' perspective against them. They see the tax collectors as sick— and therefore don't want to go near them. But Jesus says he is ministering to them as a doctor. He is dealing with their sin. The Pharisees think that sinful people are outside God's kingdom, but Jesus shows that it is those who recognize their need for a Savior who are really inside God's kingdom.

The three remaining controversies have to do with the Pharisees' religious rules. They have added manmade traditions onto God's law. So they think that Jesus and his disciples should fast (v 18-22), they think that Jesus' disciples should not pluck ears of corn on the Sabbath (v 23-28), and they think that Jesus should not heal on the Sabbath (3:1-6).

Jesus responds by showing that they need to recalibrate their understanding of what is right and wrong. You don't fast when the bridegroom is with you (2:19). The bridegroom is a reference to Jesus. He is the fixed point of reference to which every understanding of what is right and wrong must relate. Jesus uses two pictures which warn the Pharisees not to mix the old and the new (v 21-22). The old traditions of the Pharisees are stiff and brittle. Jesus is like new wine that will bust these traditions wide open. Everything must be recalibrated now that Jesus has come. Jesus makes a similar point when the Pharisees complain about his disciples plucking ears of corn on the Sabbath: "The Son of Man is lord even of the Sabbath" (v 28). Everything revolves around Jesus.

In the climax of the five conflicts (3:1-6), Jesus brings a challenge to the religious leaders. They are watching to see if he will heal a man with a withered hand on the Sabbath. Jesus asks them whether it is lawful to do good on the Sabbath. He exposes the fact that the scribes' motivation for following the rules is not love—which is the heart of God's law. Jesus heals the man, and the scribes begin to plot to have Jesus killed.

OPTIONAL EXTRA

Play Green Glass Doors. This is a talking game. The object of the game is for players to discover what can be taken through an imaginary set of green glass doors. The secret rule is that only words which include double letters (e.g. ss, oo) can be taken through the doors. Start off by saying, "I'm going through the green glass doors and I'm bringing the moon, but not the sun." Then invite the group to come up with their own ideas for what they could take through the green glass doors. Don't tell them the secret, but do give them more examples—to help them, or to confuse them! (You can also try different rules—for example, each player can only take things which begin with the same initial as

their name. Karen could take a kangaroo, and Josh could take a jumper, but not the other way around.)

GUIDANCE FOR QUESTIONS

1. What do you think people today base their sense of right and wrong on? Answers could include the following:
- What they were taught as children at school or by their family.
- What the media or social media says, or what the majority of people seem to think.
- Their own conscience and how they feel.
- The law or documents such as the Universal Declaration of Human Rights.

In today's study we'll see that Jesus is accused of doing wrong, but that he is actually the yardstick of what is right and wrong.

2. What's the scene in verses 1-4? Why do the men have to dig through the roof? Jesus is back in Capernaum, probably in the house of Peter's mother-in-law. The crowds have assembled again and filled the house to overflowing (v 2). Mark tells us that Jesus is preaching the word (v 2). The content of his preaching is not spelled out because Mark gave a summary earlier (1:15). The four men carrying the paralytic cannot get into the house to see Jesus through the door because the crowds are so great, so they climb onto the flat roof.

3. Why is Jesus' response surprising (v 5)? Most of us would worry about the damage to his host's property. But Jesus focuses on the men's faith (v 5). Then he tells the paralytic that his sins are forgiven. This is surprising because we expect him to heal the paralytic. It's also surprising because Jesus (as far as we know) has never met this man before. So it's strange that he knows his sins, and it's strange that he forgives them—it implies that Jesus sees these sins as being against himself.

- **Why do the scribes have a problem with what Jesus has said (v 6-7)?** Here is their logic: *We know God alone can forgive sins. Jesus claims to forgive sins. Therefore, Jesus is making himself out to be God. This is blasphemy!* They get the question right ("Who can forgive sins but God alone?") but their conclusion is wrong ("He is blaspheming"). They don't understand that Jesus really is God.

4. Why does healing the man prove that Jesus has authority to forgive sins (v 8-12)? Jesus asks which is easier to say: words of forgiveness or words of healing (v 9). Forgiveness is easier to say because it is invisible and internal. It is impossible to see from the outside. But physical healing is visible and external. It would be immediately evident to everyone if Jesus' word of healing failed. When Jesus heals the paralytic, he proves that he is God—he has the power of the Creator. If he is God, he has the authority to forgive sins.

5. What does the man have to do in order to be forgiven? Jesus forgives the man after seeing the faith of him and his friends (v 5). It is faith in Jesus that allows us to be forgiven, not any cleansing we could do ourselves.

6. Why is Jesus eating with the tax collectors (v 17)? Jesus turns the scribes' perspective against them. They see the tax collectors as sick—and therefore don't want to go near them. But Jesus says he is ministering to them as a doctor. He is dealing with their sin.

7. APPLY: As Jesus' followers, why is it important to keep reminding ourselves

of how much we need Jesus? Sometimes we can become too comfortable. We know we have been forgiven and so we take Jesus for granted. We can become proud and hard-hearted. We risk falling away from faith, and failing to welcome others into church.

- **As a church, how can we clearly communicate to outsiders both the seriousness of sin and the heart of Jesus to receive sinners?** Encourage the group to get practical and specific here. Think about what happens at your church gatherings when non-Christians are present; or in any other context where Christians from your church interact with non-Christians. Is it possible that anyone could think that coming to church would just make them feel worse about themselves? Is it possible that anyone could think that they are not welcome because they are not good enough, knowledgeable enough, or respectable enough? Or, on the other hand, is it possible that they could think that their sin doesn't matter and they can have all that Jesus offers while still embracing sin? If the answer is yes, what changes could you make?

8. What is the Pharisees' problem in each of these scenes (2:18, 23-4; 3:2)?
- 2:18: They think Jesus and his disciples should be fasting.
- 2:23-4: They think Jesus' disciples should not be plucking ears of corn on the Sabbath.
- 3:2: They think Jesus should not heal someone on the Sabbath.

9. How does Jesus recalibrate the question about fasting (2:19-20)? Jesus compares himself with a bridegroom. A wedding is a time of celebration and feasting. It is not a fitting time for fasting. Jesus is here, so people should celebrate.

10. If the old wineskin and cloth represent the Pharisees' traditions and the new wine and patch are Jesus' teaching, what do these pictures help us understand (v 21-22)? These pictures contain a contrast between the old and the new and a warning not to mix them together. No one fixes an old garment with a new patch of cloth because it will shrink and cause a worse tear in the old garment. No one will put new wine into an old wineskin because the new wine will expand and break the old skins. The old garment and the old wineskin are the teaching and practices of the Pharisees and scribes. These are man-made rules and man-made traditions, and they have become stiff and brittle. Jesus cannot be added to their traditions; he is like new wine that will bust their traditions wide open. His teaching is fresh. People must be prepared to follow Jesus and break free from man-made tradition.

⊗

These parables can be hard to understand. If the group is struggling, try the following questions:
• What is the problem with mixing new and old in these two pictures?
• What is the problem with mixing the Pharisees' traditions with Jesus' fresh teaching?

EXPLORE MORE
Re-read Mark 3:1-6. How does Jesus' question in verse 4 expose where the Pharisees have gone wrong? They don't care about people. They are so focused on following the rules that they have forgotten the key principle of God's law, which is always about doing good. Instead of being an expression of God's heart for his people, the Sabbath has become a competition to

see who can do nothing the best!
Why do you think they remain silent? They know that Jesus has exposed them for the frauds that they are.
What does this story show about Jesus' priorities in deciding what is right and wrong? Jesus wants to do good and to save life. He embodies God's heart to bless his people.

11. How do the Pharisees respond to what Jesus has said (v 6)? They plot to kill him. They have totally rejected his teaching.
• **But why is what Jesus has said throughout this study actually incredibly good news?** Jesus offers life (3:4)! The Pharisees want everyone to measure up to their rules in order to avoid sinning, but Jesus has the authority to forgive sins (2:10). Instead of pushing sinners away, he welcomes and transforms them.

12. APPLY: Think about the traditions, routines, and unwritten rules you have in what you do at church (in services, study groups, youth groups, or other ministries). Is there anything that you are upholding as right or wrong that could actually get in the way of people coming to Jesus? What changes could be made? You could split the group up and ask each smaller group to think about a specific ministry or regular event at your church. Could anyone get the impression that you have to be from a certain background in order to be part of your church? Or a certain type of personality, or academic ability? Another way of asking this question is to think whether you can think of any type of person who would be put off by what happens in your church

.

3 Mark 3:7 – 4:34
OUTSIDERS AND INSIDERS

THE BIG IDEA

Jesus is the only one who can make us insiders in God's kingdom. Listen to him and obey him instead of presuming on your status or making demands.

SUMMARY

What makes someone an outsider or an insider in God's kingdom? The next section of Mark develops that theme with narrative (3:7-35) and teaching (4:1-34).

In 3:7-10, many people are attracted to Jesus because of what he is doing—his healing ministry. But Jesus calls twelve disciples who will have a closer relationship with him (v 13-19). These men don't just marvel at Jesus from a distance. They live with him and are empowered by him to do the work of ministry.

Verses 20-35 show us more divergent responses to Jesus. These verses begin and end with Jesus' family, while sandwiched in between is the story of his conflict with the scribes. They accuse him of being demon-possessed, but Jesus tells them that this makes no sense. In fact he is working to defeat and bind Satan. This interaction reveals that although the scribes think Jesus is outside God's kingdom, it's really them who are outside God's kingdom. In opposing Jesus, they have aligned themselves with Satan.

Meanwhile Jesus' family—who you would expect to be insiders—also reveal themselves to be outsiders. They try to seize him, saying that he is mad (v 20-21). They seek him out and make demands of him (v 31-32). But Jesus says that his true family

are those who do the will of God.

Mark 4:1-34 develops this theme of insiders and outsiders. First Jesus tells the parable of the sower to a large crowd (v 1-9). A sower sows seed on four different soils, with different results. Later Jesus explains this parable to his disciples (v 14-20). The seed is the word of God, and the four soils are different responses.

It's significant that Jesus reveals the meaning of the parable to the twelve apostles only. He alone can reveal the secrets of the kingdom. Not everyone can easily understand what he is doing. Jesus tells his apostles that the purpose of the parables is to distinguish between insiders and outsiders (v 11-12). Outsiders in God's kingdom will hear Jesus' words but not understand them.

So how do we become insiders? By doing Jesus' will (3:35); in other words, by hearing the word, accepting it, and bearing fruit (4:20). We need Jesus to give us ears to hear, and when he does, we must use them.

Jesus is like a lamp which reveals the secrets of the kingdom (v 21-23). But we are to be careful in how we hear: the measure we use for listening will determine how much we receive (v 24-25). It is God who makes the kingdom grow (v 26-29); this may seem hidden and small at first, but one day it will be big and unmissable (v 30-32).

OPTIONAL EXTRA

Print out eight to ten famous faces, including that of the president of the US (or another head of state). Include at least one of each of the following categories:

a politician, an influential media figure, someone known for their charitable deeds, and someone known to be hostile to the president. Ask the group to put the faces in order of how likely the president is to want to have them over for dinner. Encourage debate! This introduces the theme of what makes someone an insider or an outsider in God's kingdom.

GUIDANCE FOR QUESTIONS

1. How do you become an "insider" in someone's life? What do you have to do to really get to know them? To really get to know someone, you have to spend time together. You have to listen to them and learn what they are like. You each allow the other to have an impact on you. This question introduces some of the key themes of this study: what it means to be an insider with Jesus, and what it means to listen to him well.

2. What are the differences between the crowds and the apostles in how they relate to Jesus? The crowds are attracted to Jesus because of what he is doing (v 8)—his healing ministry. We don't know how they responded to his teaching. The apostles are much closer to Jesus than the crowds. He "desired" them (v 13) and they spend lots of time just being "with him" (v 14). This is deeper and more intensive. The apostles are also empowered by Jesus. He sends the twelve disciples out to do the work of ministry as apprentices with his authority (v 14-15).

3. What are the teachers of the law accusing Jesus of (v 22)? They think he is demon-possessed. The work of Jesus must be supernatural, so they say it comes from Satan.

• **How does Jesus reveal the flaw in their logic (v 23-26)?** Jesus is saying, *How could I be extending Satan's kingdom if I am casting out demons?* A civil war in Satan's kingdom would not build it but weaken it.

4. What must Jesus be doing in order to cast out demons (v 27)? He is binding Satan and plundering his house.

• **And what are the scribes doing when they accuse him of having an evil spirit (v 29-30)?** Their accusation is not a momentary mistake, but an eternal sin: a blasphemy against the Holy Spirit. They are calling the Holy Spirit (by whom Jesus does his miracles) an evil spirit.

5. Look at the start and end of the passage (v 20-21, 31-35). Where do you think Jesus' family stand—are they inside or outside the kingdom? Why? Jesus' family want to claim him. They try to "seize" him because they think he is mad (v 21). This is just a less extreme version of what the scribes have said. Jesus' mother and brothers need to recognize that Jesus' claim over them is stronger than their claim over him. They want him to do what they want. But members of his true family (insiders in his kingdom) do what he wants (v 35). The family of Jesus are close to Jesus physically, but they are not yet insiders.

6. APPLY: What would it look like to respond like the following people today?
• **The crowds:** We might be attracted to Jesus without really understanding what he came for. We're solely interested in what he can do for us, rather than wanting to obey him and glorify him.

• **The scribes:** We might totally reject

Jesus and not listen properly to him. (Please note: people with a tender conscience often worry they may have committed this unforgiveable sin. But anyone who is worried that they have committed this sin has not committed it—because that very anxiety itself shows a sensitivity to repent and seek forgiveness. The eternal sin is perpetual unbelief—calling what Jesus does "evil." In that state, forgiveness can never come, because forgiveness is only found by embracing Jesus as the Son of God.)

- **Jesus' mother and brothers:** We might assert our rights over Jesus, making demands of him and assuming that he is ours to command, while not actually obeying him.

- **How can we make sure we respond like the apostles instead?** The apostles live with Jesus. They spend lots of time with him, learning to be like him. We have the same opportunity. Jesus promised he would be with us always, even to the end of the age (Matthew 28:20). Jesus is with us and we must learn to cultivate our fellowship with him. This means being disciplined about pursuing time with him, reading his word and relating to him in prayer. It's surprisingly easy to effectively tell Jesus to go away because we have to answer emails.

7. What are the four types of soil, and what responses to Jesus' preaching do these represent (v 2-8, 14-20)?
- The path (v 4) represents a hardened heart—so hardened that the word has no effect. Satan comes and snatches the seed away (v 15). These people immediately reject the teaching of Jesus.
- The rocky ground (v 5-6) has shallow soil. These people receive the word joyfully,

but not deeply (v 16-17). Their shallow reception of the word means that when suffering comes, they fall away and stop following Jesus.
- The thorny ground (v 7) represents those whose hearts are worldly: crowded with desires, worries, and lies (v 19). These things choke the word, so that these people do not become followers of Jesus.
- The good soil (v 8) is anyone who hears the word and accepts it. They endure in their embrace of Jesus' message, and bear fruit as a result (v 20).

8. Which "soils" do you think are represented by the various people we saw in Mark 3?
- The scribes are like the path. They immediately oppose the teaching of Jesus.
- The apostles are good soil. They are following Jesus, learning from him, and working on his behalf—bearing fruit in the lives of others.
- Jesus' mother and brothers may be like the thorny soil. They want Jesus, but they have their own agenda. (Later, however, we know that Jesus' brother James became the leader of the church in Jerusalem. He at least proved to be good soil!)
- The crowds could be like the rocky soil. They are attracted to Jesus, but we have seen no evidence that they really take his message to heart.

9. Who does Jesus explain the parable to (v 10)? A specific group: the twelve apostles plus others who are close to Jesus.

10. Why does he use parables and not explain them clearly to everyone (v 11-12)? The parables create two categories of people: insiders and outsiders. The outsiders get only the parables. The insiders hear the same parables as the outsiders, but they are given something extra—how to interpret them. Jesus reveals the secrets of the kingdom to his disciples as his true family.

EXPLORE MORE
Read Mark 4:21-34.
The lamp in verses 21-22 is Jesus. What does this parable tell us about how we can find out the secrets of the kingdom? Jesus reveals the secrets of the kingdom to us.

What does the parable of the measure (v 24-25) call us to do? To listen well. The bigger the jug you use, the more oil you'll get. The more we listen to Jesus, the more we'll receive.

What does the parable of the growing seed (v 26-29) tell us about how God's kingdom grows? God is the one who brings the growth.

What does the parable of the mustard seed (v 30-32) tell us about why Jesus' work seems small or hidden at first? The kingdom has a deceptively small beginning, but it will conclude with a large ending. Jesus was born in a manger and died on a cross. This seems unimpressive and hidden. But one day Jesus will come again on the clouds of heaven with all the angels. That second coming will be big and obvious and overpowering.

11. Who are the insiders in God's kingdom, according to what you have read in this study? Insiders are those who heed Jesus' command to "hear the word and accept it and bear fruit" (v 20)—in other words, those who listen to Jesus and do his will (3:35). Jesus is the one who must open our hearts and our ears to his words. But we also have the responsibility to listen and obey.

12. APPLY: In what ways can we hear Jesus' words but not really listen to them? How can we avoid this? We might listen to Jesus' words to begin with, but when life becomes hard, we stop reading his word and going to him in prayer—like the rocky ground. Or we might listen to Jesus on a Sunday, but not really put his words into practice in the rest of the week—like the thorny ground. The way to avoid this is to have deep roots in Jesus! We should actively pursue companionship with him through reading his word and hearing it preached, through prayer and worship, and through fellowship with other Christians. We should seek to put his word into practice every day.

Mark 4:35 – 5:43

4 FEAR AND FAITH

THE BIG IDEA

Jesus is not only powerful but also merciful and compassionate. When we are afraid, we can run to him.

SUMMARY

Faith is the major theme of the story in 4:35-41. Evening has come and Jesus and his disciples set off in a boat to go to the other side of the lake where Jesus has been teaching. A windstorm arises and the disciples fear for their lives. But Jesus is asleep. They wake him, asking whether he cares. They want to trust Jesus, but the storm looks deadly. Jesus tells the storm to be still, and the wind and waves obey. The disciples are now afraid for a different reason as they begin to wonder who Jesus really is.

On the other side of the lake, Jesus encounters a man possessed by demons (5:1-20). No one has the strength to subdue this man's violence, but when he meets Jesus he falls down in fearful recognition that Jesus is stronger. The demons beg to be sent into a herd of pigs. They go down as the pigs drown in the sea.

The local people come to see what has happened. They respond the same way as the disciples in the previous story: with fear. They beg Jesus to leave. But the man who has been freed from the demons begs to be with Jesus—the right thing to beg for.

These two stories reveal Jesus' power as the divine Son of God. He does what no one else can do. But we are meant to respond with faith, not fear. We are meant to beg him not to leave our lives, but to stay.

5:21-43 features a sandwich: one story inside another. A ruler of the synagogue comes to Jesus in the same way as the demoniac: he falls at Jesus' feet and begs for help. His daughter is dying and he asks Jesus to heal her.

The middle of the sandwich comes next (v 25-34). A woman in the crowd has a disease which no one can heal. She has heard the reports about Jesus and believes that he can do what no one else can do. She touches the edge of his garments and then retreats into the shadows. But Jesus knows that a healing has happened. He asks, "Who touched my garments?" The disciples don't understand why Jesus is asking this question, but it becomes clear that he is drawing the woman out. She has been an outsider because of her disease, but he wants to free her from shame. He calls her "Daughter" and tells her that her faith has made her well.

The sandwich concludes in verses 35-43. Someone rushes up to Jairus to tell him his daughter is dead. Mark wants us to feel the drama of this moment. Jesus has stopped, apparently needlessly, and now the little girl is dead. But Jesus tells Jairus to have faith. He should believe that Jesus can still answer his request. Jesus goes and heals the girl. He speaks tenderly to her and makes sure she is fed.

Jesus can do what no one else can do. He is stronger than demons, stronger than disease, stronger than death. But the strength of his love shines even brighter. In these stories we see that Jesus is not only powerful but also full of mercy and love.

OPTIONAL EXTRA

What's the scariest thing that's ever happened to someone in the group? Invite a few people to tell their stories. Give a prize to the best storyteller!

GUIDANCE FOR QUESTIONS

1. What might make a person seem scary—or not scary at all? This is a warm-up question and there is no right or wrong answer!

2. In the first story (4:35-41), Jesus asks the disciples why they are afraid. Why shouldn't they be? Jesus asks, "Have you still no faith?" (v 40). He is God—the disciples should know that they can trust him! Jesus demonstrates that he is in control first by being fast asleep in the middle of the storm (v 38) and then by calming the storm (v 39).

- **But why are they still afraid in verse 41?** Jesus just shattered their pre-existing categories. They think Jesus is the Messiah. But Jesus' control over the storm makes them wonder if he is even more than the Messiah. Are they meeting their Maker in that boat?

3. When other people have met the demon-possessed man, what has happened (5:3-4)? People have tried to subdue or tame him by chaining him up, but no one has managed it.

- **What's different about his encounter with Jesus (v 6-13)?**
  - Since people have tried to chain the man up, we might expect him to attack Jesus. But he falls down in fearful recognition that Jesus is stronger (v 6).
  - Jesus does not need to bind the man up or tame him. He transforms him—releasing him from the demons (v 8, 13).

EXPLORE MORE
Read Isaiah 65:1-4

What details can you spot in Isaiah 65 that are relevant to this situation [in Mark 5]?

- "I was ready to be found by those who did not seek me" (v 1): the demon-possessed man does not seek Jesus out, and since he is a Gentile he is probably not seeking the God of Israel in any other way either.
- "…who sit in tombs, and spend the night in secret places" (v 4): this is a description of what the demon-possessed man was doing.
- "…who eat pig's flesh" (v 5): Gentiles ate meat from pigs, unlike Jews, to whom it was forbidden.

What is God's attitude to these people (Isaiah 65:1)? God is ready to be found by these people. He is available to them.

How does Jesus exemplify this attitude? Jesus deliberately goes into Gentile territory. He makes himself available to non-Jews.

4. The crowds can see that Jesus is powerful. How do they respond (v 17)? They beg Jesus to leave the region.

- **Why do you think the formerly demon-possessed man responds differently (v 18)?** This man has been transformed by Jesus. He recognizes how much Jesus has done for him, and therefore longs to be with him. He doesn't just see Jesus' power, but also his purpose: he is the Messiah who comes to deliver people and plunder Satan's kingdom.

5. Jesus wants the man to tell people about his power—and what else (v 19)? His mercy. This is the goodness and love of God toward those who are in misery or distress. Jesus is not just powerful but also willing to use that power to help us.

6. APPLY: Jesus' mercy calls us to mission. What could you say about "how much the Lord has done for you and how he has had mercy on you" this week—and to whom? Invite the group to think specifically about their own testimony of God's goodness in their lives. This should include Jesus' death for their sins on the cross, but also more personal stories of how they came to faith or of particular moments when they were aware of God's mercy and forgiveness. What difference has Jesus made to their lives? Encourage the group to think how they could articulate that to someone who does not yet believe.

7. What do you think Jairus believes about Jesus (v 22-23)? Jairus expects Jesus to make his daughter well (v 23). He knows he is powerful and expects him to be kind.

- **What about the woman in the crowd (v 28)?** She has heard reports about Jesus and knows that he can make her well (v 27-28). Like Jairus, she believes that Jesus is powerful. However, she is ashamed. She just wants to touch the edge of his garment from behind and then make a quick getaway. She doesn't seem to believe that he would want to help her.

8. Why is Jesus' question in verse 30 surprising (v 31)? Lots of people have touched Jesus: everyone is pressing in on him. It doesn't make sense to ask who touched him.

- **Why do you think he asks it? What's the result (v 33)?** Jesus wants to draw the woman out. This woman was an outsider always living in the shadows of society. So he forces her to come in front of everyone. He knows what she needs and shows her great tenderness.

9. What does the impact seem to have been on Jairus' faith in Jesus? Jesus commands Jairus to have faith (v 36). So Jairus must think his last hope is gone.

10. What do you think Jairus would have said about Jesus by the end of the story, and why?
- Jesus is amazing. "They were immediately overcome with amazement" (v 42).
- Jesus is powerful. He can do what no one else can do—raise someone from the dead!
- Jesus doesn't make mistakes. He knew what he was doing when he stopped to speak to the woman in the crowd.
- Jesus is kind. He addresses the girl as "Talitha" which means "little girl" (v 41). This girl is 12 years old (v 42)—not that little! It is a term of affection. Jesus also shows that he cares for every little detail of the girl's life when he tells her parents that in their amazement they should not forget to feed her (v 43).

11. In 4:41, the disciples were afraid because they saw that Jesus could do what no one else can do. Imagine you had witnessed the events of Mark 5 and were now talking to the disciples. What would you say about Jesus? How would you encourage them to respond with faith instead of fear? Jesus is God: he is stronger than anything or anyone else. But the strength of his love shines even brighter. Jesus treats his people with unspeakable tenderness. He addresses both the woman in the crowd and Jairus' daughter with great affection (v 34, 41). He sees what each individual person needs. The right response is that of the man who was possessed by demons: to beg to be with Jesus.

12. APPLY: What help does what you

have read give us for situations that seem impossible, or for times when we are afraid? Jesus is powerful, merciful, and compassionate. We can always run to him in prayer. Throughout Mark's Gospel, people who recognize that they need Jesus' help and fall before his feet are the ones who receive mercy, healing, and freedom. So in any situation, we can beg Jesus to do what only he can do. We can rely upon him and rest in him.

5 CLEAN AND UNCLEAN

Mark 7:1-37

THE BIG IDEA

Jesus has high standards: when we sin, we are unclean. But Jesus also welcomes unclean people and makes them clean. When we sin, we can come to him and be made new.

SUMMARY

We are in the middle of a long section of signs which reveal Jesus' identity (4:35 – 8:21). There is a rhythm of bread miracles and boat miracles, which we'll look at in the next study. But for now we'll focus on chapter 7 and the theme of clean and unclean.

The Pharisees are once again attacking Jesus (v 1-5). They believe that his disciples should be washing their hands more. This was not just a hygiene issue. It was a question of ritual purity. People believed that if you did not wash hands, cups, and vessels before eating, you would be "unclean" before God—unworthy to enter his presence. The Pharisees are basically saying that Jesus doesn't care about the holiness of God. They think that his standards are much lower than God's standards.

But Jesus says they are hypocrites (v 6-13). Their ritual scrupulousness could make it

look like they are serious about drawing near to God, but really their hearts are far from God. They are sharing man-made ideas and treating them as if they are commandments from God—in such a way that they actually cause others to break God's commandments. People justify failing to care for their parents by saying that their money or possessions are "Corban"—devoted to God. They invoke God's name to avoid doing something God himself commanded.

Jesus next explains that defilement is not an outside to inside issue, but an inside to outside issue (v 14-23). Purity and holiness are issues of the heart, not the stomach—so food cannot defile people, only what is in their hearts. The Pharisees think they are clean, but they have rotten hearts.

Jesus travels to the region of Tyre—a Gentile region, where Jewish customs were not followed (v 24). A woman has a little daughter with an unclean spirit. She is a definite outsider. Even Jewish women did not approach Jewish rabbis. And Gentiles were not supposed to do so, either— certainly not Gentile women who had a daughter with an unclean spirit! This woman would have had three strikes against her in the Pharisees' eyes. However, the woman begs Jesus to help her (v 26).

Jesus' response seems offensive at first glance. He tells her that Gentiles are like dogs under the table, while Jews are like children. The Jews should be fed first. What Jesus means is that there is an order to his mission. He came to show Israel that he is the fulfillment of all that God promised to Israel. After his resurrection, Jesus would send his disciples to make disciples of all the nations. But not yet—right now the Gentiles had to wait their turn.

The woman understands and agrees (v 28). She recognizes that she should not have a place at the table. But she also knows that there is more than enough for Israel. If she is a dog, she can eat the crumbs that the children have rejected. Because of this response, she receives the answer to her request (v 29-30).

This story turns the tables on the Pharisees' assumptions about what makes someone clean or unclean. Everyone would have regarded this woman as unclean. But Jesus accepts her and releases her daughter from the unclean spirit. Jesus takes what is unclean and makes it clean.

The final story in Mark 7 involves a deaf man—again, a Gentile (v 31-37). Jesus uses a kind of sign language to tell the man what he is going to do. Then he heals him.

OPTIONAL EXTRA

Set the group (or one volunteer) a clean/unclean challenge. Present each person with a ball of some kind, placed on a piece of plain paper or a white sheet, and some (washable!) paint. Using fingers, paintbrushes, or any other implements you choose, they must cover the ball with as much paint as possible, while keeping the white paper as clean as possible.

GUIDANCE FOR QUESTIONS

1. What's the dirtiest you've ever been? What did being dirty stop you from doing? This question should draw out some interesting stories! When we're dirty, we usually don't want to touch anything clean—or other people don't want us to! This is a way of introducing the group to the key concept in this session.

2. What traditions are Jesus' disciples ignoring (v 1-5)? Jewish traditions about washing. This tradition, although not part of the Old Testament law as such (except for priests and for food offered in the temple—see Exodus 30:17-21; Numbers 18:8-13), had become so intertwined with Jewish religion that people believed "to be Jewish" is to wash hands, cups, and vessels before eating. Mark specifically mentions the fact that they would wash after coming from the marketplace (Mark 7:4)—which is where Jesus has just been performing miracles (6:56).

3. How does Jesus assess the Pharisees' traditions (v 6-8)?
- They are hypocritical (v 6). The Pharisees' ritual scrupulousness could look like they are serious about drawing near to God, but Jesus says that their hearts are far from God. The motivation for their rule-keeping is not love for God but a desire to be seen by others.
- They are "the tradition of men" (v 8): they don't come from God. In fact, they actually cause people to break the commandments of God.

4. What is more important than external rituals or words (v 6)? The heart. True worship of God comes from within, not external things.

5. What can make a person unclean, in fact (v 15, 20-23)? What comes out of a person is what defiles them. That is, "evil thoughts, sexual immorality, theft, murder, adultery, coveting, wickedness, deceit, sensuality, envy, slander, pride, foolishness" (v 20-22). These sins arise from within us.

6. APPLY: In what ways can we fall into the trap of honoring God externally while being far from him internally? How could we avoid this?

• We can honor God with our lips— speaking about him as if we love him—yet be hypocrites with hearts that do not really love him. We need to assess our own words about God: do we really believe them? Are we really living in a way that is consistent with them?

• We can obey all God's rules—living moral lives, going to church, and so on—yet not have hearts that truly worship him. We need to assess our own motives: are we just following rules, or are we motivated by love? We need to keep coming back to the truth that we are sinners in need of a Savior, and ask for the help of the Holy Spirit to sanctify us, rather than just trying to keep the rules in our own strength.

7. What do you think the Pharisees would have thought of the Syrophoenician woman (v 25-26)? Would they have wanted Jesus to go near her? This woman has three strikes against her. She is a Gentile and a woman (even Jewish women did not approach Jewish rabbis) and she has a daughter with an unclean spirit. The Pharisees would not have approved!

8. How does Jesus acknowledge the difference between Jews and Gentiles (v 27)? Jews are like children—they are

God's chosen people—while Gentiles are like the dogs beneath the table.

9. What are the woman's expectations about how Jesus will treat Gentiles (v 28)? She accepts Jesus' words, recognizing that she does not have a place at the table because she is not from Israel. But she also knows that there is more than enough for Israel. She expects Jesus to give to the Gentiles what the Israelites have rejected.

10. What is it that makes the woman clean? It's not external things that make us clean, but internal things. She is clean because she is full of faith.

11. What happens to the woman's daughter and why (v 30)? She is made clean—the demon leaves her. This is because of her mother's response of faith in Jesus.

EXPLORE MORE
Read Mark 7:31-37
What does that [Jesus' use of sign language] tell us about Jesus' attitude toward the man? He acts with tender attention and mercy. He sees not just the man's problem but the man himself.
What do people conclude about Jesus (v 37)? "He has done all things well."

12. APPLY: Based on everything you've read in the study, what should we do when we have sinned?

• We should take sin seriously. Jesus has high standards. Sin defiles us (v 15, 23): it matters.

• We should ask Jesus boldly for forgiveness. He is able to cleanse us!

6

HARD HEARTS

THE BIG IDEA

Jesus reveals himself to us—yet it is so easy to respond with a hard heart. Instead we must respond worshipfully and trustfully.

SUMMARY

The twelve apostles have been sent out to teach about Jesus, cast out demons, and heal the sick (see 6:7-13). As they return, we begin the story of the feeding of the 5,000 (v 30-44). The disciples and Jesus go away to a secluded destination to rest, but they find a great crowd waiting for them. Seeing the people stirs Jesus to the core with compassion. He sees that they are like sheep without a shepherd. This is a quotation from Moses (Numbers 27:17). Jesus provides the teaching they need, but he also provides for them physically. It becomes late in the day, and they need food. The disciples point out that they don't have the kind of money it would take to purchase enough food for all these people. But Jesus organizes the people into groups, takes the small amount of food that they do have, and starts giving it out. The result is that all the people eat and are satisfied.

This story has many parallels with the story of God's provision of manna for his people in the wilderness (Exodus 16).

Next we see a boat miracle (v 45-52). The crowds have been dismissed and Jesus has gone away up the mountain alone, while the disciples get into the boat to cross the lake. But the wind is against the disciples. Jesus sees them struggling and goes out to them—without a boat. He walks on the water.

Mark tells us that "he meant to pass by them" (v 48). This is another biblical echo. This is exactly what God did for both Moses and Elijah: he passed by them so they could see his glory (Exodus 33:19; 1 Kings 19:11). He was revealing his identity—which is what Jesus is doing here. "It is I," he says (Mark 6:50). In the original language this is the same phrase that God used to declare his name to Moses: "I AM" (Exodus 34:5-7—it's translated there "the LORD"). Jesus is revealing himself to his disciples. He is saying, *Do not fear, because I am God!*

These miracles are like repetitions of moments in the Old Testament. But the disciples do not understand that. They don't see what Jesus is revealing about his identity. They have hard hearts (Mark 6:52).

Next we skip forwards to a second bread miracle. The story in 8:1-10 is very similar to the story of the feeding of the 5,000. So the disciples' memory should kick in at this point. They should expect Jesus to perform a similar miracle. Disappointingly, they don't.

The story follows the same pattern. All the people eat and are satisfied, and the disciples pick up the leftovers. Once again we have a sign that Jesus is the Son of God. Which is why it is so jarring to immediately overhear the Pharisees' demand for a sign from heaven (v 11-13). They are seeking to test him. Jesus sighs—grieving against them and their unbelief—and refuses to give them a sign.

Mark now brings this first half of his Gospel to a climax with a story of bread in the boat (v 14-21). Jesus warns the disciples about the leaven of the Pharisees and the leaven of Herod. The disciples do not understand—

they think he is commenting on their lack of physical bread. But in fact this "leaven" is the response of unbelief. The disciples must not reject the true identity of Jesus as the divine Son of God, as Herod and the Pharisees have done.

To hammer this point home, Jesus asks the disciples if they are really insiders. They have seen all the signs. But do they really have eyes that see or ears that hear? "Do you not yet understand?" he asks them (v 21).

It's easy to look at the disciples and feel smug. How could they keep forgetting the things that Jesus has done? But the question comes right back at us. Too often we act as if we've forgotten who Jesus is. We should pray for soft hearts and keep reminding ourselves of Jesus' identity.

OPTIONAL EXTRA

Get hold of some "magic towels." These are flannels compressed into small, hard shapes. When you put them in water they expand into soft towels. You could use these to help you reflect and pray at the end of the session. Give each group member a magic towel and invite them to put it into a bowl of water. As it turns from hard to soft, they can pray that God would remove any hardness in their hearts.

GUIDANCE FOR QUESTIONS

1. How forgetful are you? When does forgetfulness not really matter? When does it? This question is designed to get people talking. In this study we'll see that the disciples are surprisingly forgetful about who Jesus is and what he can do.

2. What does Jesus think and feel about the crowds (v 34)? He has compassion on them, because they are like sheep without a shepherd.

3. In Mark 6:30-52, how is Jesus like a shepherd? They are in a desolate place, on a mountain—the type of place a shepherd might take his sheep. More importantly, Jesus satisfies his sheep—providing both spiritual food (v 34) and physical food (v 41-42). He is their leader, their guide, and their provider.

4. Look at Exodus 16:1-4, 13-16. This is another part of Moses' story. What links can you spot with the feeding of the 5,000? The setting is desolate (Exodus 16:1; Mark 6:32). The people need food (Exodus 16:3; Mark 6:35-36). In Exodus, God provides food—enough for everyone (Exodus 16:4, 14). In Mark, Jesus provides food—more than enough for everyone (Mark 6:42-43)!

5. The scene changes in verses 45-48. Where are the disciples and where is Jesus now? Jesus is praying alone on the mountain, while the disciples are in the boat on the lake below.

6. Why do you think Jesus is repeating these moments from the Old Testament? Jesus is revealing his identity. He is God—the God of the Old Testament.

• **What don't the disciples understand? Why not?** They see the miracle but miss its whole point. They don't see that Jesus is God. Their hearts are hardened (v 52).

7. APPLY: Today Jesus reveals to us by his word and through his Spirit. What would it look like to read the Bible with a hard heart, even as a believer? What attitude should we have instead? Sometimes we read the Bible simply as a cerebral exercise, or in order to commend ourselves to God. But God is the divine author, and he reveals himself through his word. We should read the Bible worshipfully, knowing that he is revealing himself to us there. We should respond with worship, awe, and faith.

8. What does the situation in 8:1-4 have in common with the one in 6:30-38?

- The setting is the same—a desolate place (6:32; 8:4).
- There is a large crowd, with people from lots of different places. They are not close to people's homes (6:33-34; 8:3).
- Jesus' same heart of compassion is on display (6:34; 8:2).
- Food is needed for the crowds (6:36; 8:2-3).
- The disciples don't know how to solve this problem (6:37; 8:4).

9. Look at verses 11-13. Why do you think Jesus sighs at the Pharisees? Jesus

is grieving about their unbelief. He has just performed a sign, but now they demand another one—not because they need one, but because they want to test him. Jesus will not give them a sign for that reason.

10. If "the leaven of the Pharisees" means responding to Jesus like the Pharisees do, what is Jesus warning the disciples against? The Pharisees are putting

Jesus to the test. They are trying to trap him. The "leaven of the Pharisees" means responding with similar unbelief.

11. How does their response show that they are already falling into that trap (v 16-21)? The disciples hear the word

"leaven" and think that Jesus is commenting on their lack of physical bread (v 14-16). They have not understood Jesus' words about the Pharisees and Herod. They have also not understood what Jesus was revealing about himself in the two bread miracles (v 18-21).

Their response is fundamentally one of unbelief. They are blind and deaf and their hearts are hard (v 17-18).

EXPLORE MORE
Read Mark 6:18-29
What did Herod think about John

(v 20)? He feared John as a righteous and holy man. He wanted to hear him, but he didn't understand his teaching.

What did he do to him in the end

(v 27-28)? He had him beheaded.

What got in the way of his fragile belief

(v 21-26)? Herod feared losing face with his family and dinner guests more than he feared John. He feared man more than God and loved sin too much to let go and repent.

Read Mark 6:14-16
Why is Herod's response to Jesus better than the Pharisees'? And in another sense, why is it just as bad? Herod seems

to believe that Jesus comes from God. He thinks he is John resurrected, and he thought that John was a holy man. But he still comes to the wrong conclusion and rejects the true identity of Jesus as the divine Son of God.

So what do you think "the leaven of Herod" is? Like the response of the

Pharisees, it is a response of unbelief.

12. APPLY: In what ways can we, even as believers, end up acting as if we've forgotten who Jesus is?

- We can panic and doubt when hard times come instead of trusting in Jesus' plans.
- We can be tempted into testing Jesus and questioning him—having a cynical response rather than a worshipful one.
- We can be seduced by sin and pursue our own pleasures instead of knowing Jesus.

- **What should we pray for our hearts?** We should pray that Jesus will remove our hard hearts and give us soft ones that know, love, and worship him.

7 Mark 8:22 – 10:52
TRUE GREATNESS

THE BIG IDEA

Jesus is the king of glory, yet he also came to suffer. A true understanding of Jesus will lead us to a true understanding of what it means to follow him: we are to be servants of all.

SUMMARY

This next section of Mark follows Jesus and his disciples as they journey to Jerusalem. It begins and ends with the healing of a blind man. These bookends are about physical blindness, but the stories in the middle are about spiritual blindness. This journey to Jerusalem is actually a struggle for sight.

Jesus seems to take two attempts to heal the man's blindness in 8:22-26. But this is actually a parable, an object lesson. The blind man represents the disciples, whose spiritual sight is only partial. Others don't see who Jesus is (v 27-28), but Peter sees that Jesus is the Christ—God's promised Messiah. Yet when Jesus tells the disciples that he is going to suffer and die and rise again, Peter rebukes him (v 31-33). He has just declared that Jesus is the Messiah, but he does not understand what being a Messiah is all about. Jesus will not fit earthly expectations. He is indeed a king who will one day come in glory, but he is also one who carries a cross. Not only this, but those who follow him will also have to carry a cross (v 34-38).

The next scene gives us a glimpse of the glorious future that is promised to those who follow Jesus (9:1-13). Peter, James, and John get to see the divine power and glory of Jesus on display. Yet they are still only partially sighted—they can't connect the dots of Jesus' death and resurrection.

After casting an unclean spirit out of a boy (v 14-29), Jesus teaches on various topics (9:30 – 10:31). We focus on two episodes in which he talks about true greatness. Jesus keeps talking about his death and resurrection (9:31; 10:33-34), but the disciples are more interested in their own greatness.

In the first scene (9:30-37), Jesus gives them a lesson in humility. He explains that true greatness in God's kingdom means being the servant of all. He uses a child to reinforce the lesson. A child is not important by worldly standards and cannot do anything for the disciples. But the criteria for receiving someone isn't their worth, but Jesus' worth. When they receive a child in Jesus' name, they are really receiving him. So serving the lowly is about accepting Jesus.

In the second scene (10:32-45), James and John ask to be given positions of power when Jesus comes in glory. Jesus does not rebuke their quest for greatness but redefines what greatness means. For worldly rulers, greatness is about gaining power and position over others. But the true standard of greatness is Jesus—who came not to get but to give. If we want to know what greatness is, we should look to him.

This section of Mark closes with another story about a blind man. Bartimaeus recognizes who Jesus is (v 47) and his request for sight is granted (v 51-52). This man sees Jesus rightly and responds rightly: he follows Jesus on the road toward the cross.

OPTIONAL EXTRA

Find some optical illusions online and test your vision. This illustrates how you can see something, yet not see it perfectly!

GUIDANCE FOR QUESTIONS

1. What big desires or hopes do you have for your future? Why? In this study we will see the disciples craving greatness. Similarly, many of us have big ambitions for our future careers. For others, it may be less about greatness and more about happiness or security. For example, group members may desire marriage, children, a house, or good health. Or they may have ambitions for their children's futures more than their own.

2. What is strange about the healing of the blind man (v 22-25)? Jesus seems to take two attempts to heal the man's blindness.

3. What does Peter see clearly about Jesus (v 27-29)? He says that he is the Christ: God's promised Messiah.

4. What does he rebuke Jesus for and why (v 31-33)? Jesus has just said that the Son of Man—that is, God's promised king (see Daniel 7:13-14)—will suffer and die. Peter does not like this. He thinks that as the Christ, Jesus should go and defeat his enemies, not be killed by them. Peter has just declared that Jesus is the Messiah, yet in the next moment, he is telling Jesus that he does not understand what being a Messiah is all about. Peter has his mind set on the things of man (v 33). Jesus will not fit earthly expectations. Peter needs to embrace God's plans instead of his own.

(NOTE: Why does Jesus call Peter "Satan"? Doesn't that seem a little harsh? I think the answer is fairly simple. Satan once offered Jesus a shortcut—he could have all the kingdoms of the world, without going to the cross (Matthew 4:8-9; Luke 4:5-7). Peter's "teaching" is taking a page right out of that playbook.)

5. How should seeing the truth about Jesus affect his followers' lives (v 34)? Not only will Jesus die on a cross, but those who follow him will also have to carry a cross. He calls us to deny ourselves—to say "no" to some of our deepest longings. Instead of pursuing what seems right to ourselves, we should pursue the way of loss and sacrifice, like Jesus.

- **Why? What is the warning and what is the promise in this text (v 35-38)?**
  - You might be so wildly successful in your quest to say "yes" to yourself that you end up gaining the whole world. But in doing so you will lose your life (or your soul, as some translations have it, v 36). The truth is that all ways other than following Jesus lead to death.
  - Jesus says that if we are ashamed of him and his words, he will be ashamed of us (v 38).
  - Don't miss the promise in this text, though. The cost of discipleship is connected to Jesus. Jesus calls us to lose our lives "for my sake" (v 35). We deny lesser things to get greater things. Jesus is saying, *As you deny yourself, you find your real self and eternal life in me.* Following Jesus is never mainly about what you lose, but what you gain forever. Jesus will one day come in glory (v 38), and his followers will be part of that glory too.

EXPLORE MORE
Read Mark 9:1-13
What are Peter, James, and John seeing (v 1)? The kingdom of God coming in power.

What do they literally see (v 2-4)? Jesus' appearance changes, making his clothes more radiantly white than anyone on earth could bleach them. This is the divine power and glory of our Lord Jesus Christ on display! Moses and Elijah appear with him.

Why does Peter need to hear the statement and the command in verse 7? Peter already knows that Jesus is the Messiah. But it's not clear that he realizes that he is actually God's Son. Peter rebuked Jesus and tried to tell him what to do and be. Instead he should listen to him and worship him as God's Son.

But what do the disciples fail to understand (v 9-10)? They still can't connect the dots of Jesus' death and resurrection.

6. APPLY: What could it look like for us to deny ourselves for Jesus' sake today?

- Denying ourselves means saying no to sin. Jesus has already taught what it looks like to follow our sinful hearts: "For from within, out of the heart of man, come evil thoughts, sexual immorality, theft, murder, adultery, coveting, wickedness, deceit, sensuality, envy, slander, pride, foolishness" (7:21-23).

- Denying ourselves means putting Jesus before ourselves—prioritising him. This might involve speaking about our faith when we'd rather keep quiet; setting aside time for prayer or Bible reading even when we are busy; going to church meetings when we'd rather not; caring for others and prioritising others' needs; giving money to the work of God's kingdom; and many other things!

7. What does Jesus keep on saying about himself (9:30-31; 10:33-34)? He is going to be arrested and put to death, and then he will rise again.

8. What are the disciples more concerned about (9:34; 10:37)? Their own greatness!

9. What makes someone great, according to 9:35-37? Being greater than all in God's kingdom means being servant of all.

- **What example of this does Jesus give, and what motive does he provide?** The disciples should welcome children. A child is not important by worldly standards of the time and cannot do anything for them. But the criteria for receiving someone isn't their worth, but Jesus' worth. When they receive a child in Jesus' name, they are really receiving him. So serving the lowly is about accepting Jesus.

10. What two different standards of greatness does Jesus describe in 10:42-45? For worldly rulers, greatness is about gaining power and position over others. But the true standard of greatness is Jesus. The Son of Man is Lord over all, but he did not come to lord it over all. He came not to get but to give. If we want to know what greatness is, we should look to him.

11. APPLY: Who are you "greater" than, according to the world's standards? What can you do to serve them? Encourage the group to think of specific individuals. Perhaps a subordinate at work, a friend who is less "successful" in some way, or a younger person. Think of practical ways you could serve those individuals and put them first.

12. APPLY: Think back to the ambitions and hopes you discussed at the start of the study. How does what you've seen in this study change your perspective or priorities? True greatness means serving others and bringing glory to Jesus. Encourage the group to think about how their ambitions and hopes for the future fit into that. Is there any way in which they are seeking their own greatness more than Jesus'? Is there any way in which they are prioritising other things above Jesus? How could their ambitions and hopes contribute to the building of Jesus' kingdom?

---

8 Mark 11:11 – 12:44
JESUS IN THE TEMPLE

THE BIG IDEA

Jesus came to challenge hypocrisy and show us what it really means to honor God. He calls us to truly devote ourselves to God rather than just going through the motions.

SUMMARY

Jesus is now in Jerusalem. He is hungry, but the fig tree he spots has no fruit. He utters a curse: "May no one ever eat fruit from you again" (11:14). This is not a case of childish anger. Jesus is acting out a parable based on Jeremiah 8:13. Jeremiah described the people as being like a fig tree with no figs: they had not grown or borne fruit but had rejected what God gave them. They were therefore bound for judgment.

This scene makes sense of the next story (v 15-19): Jesus is cursing the temple, just as he cursed the fig tree. He enters the temple and drives out those who are selling and buying. Jesus is effectively stopping the temple from functioning. He says, "You have made it a den of robbers" (v 17). This phrase comes from Jeremiah 7:9-11. The people in Jeremiah's day were coming into the temple because they believed it would keep them safe from God's judgment and allow them to keep sinning—instead of coming in genuine repentance and asking for forgiveness. They were like robbers hiding in a cave. The people in Jesus' day are doing the same thing.

The disciples pass the fig tree again and see that it has withered as a result of Jesus' curse (Mark 11:20-21). Jesus now unpacks the nature of prayer for his disciples (v 22-25). Prayer is not a matter of external ritual or liturgy or location. It must come from a heart full of faith, and full of forgiveness. This is how we should come to God—not through empty sacrifices.

11:27 – 12:44 describe Jesus' third trip to the temple and a series of disputes with the religious teachers there. We focus on the last question Jesus is asked (12:28-34). A scribe asks Jesus which commandment is the most important. Jesus replies that we should love God and love others. He commends the scribe's response that these things are more important than temple sacrifices. Making offerings is meaningless without love for God: that's the main thing.

Jesus now makes some challenges of his own. He first calls into question the scribes' understanding of the Messiah (v 35-37). Next he tells a cautionary tale about what the scribes do (v 38-40). They are a picture of fake devotion to God. What seems like devotion is actually self-promotion. Moreover, they take advantage of the vulnerable. Jesus says they will be condemned. Finally, Jesus paints a contrasting picture of true devotion (v 41-44). He has already shown the spiritual bankruptcy of ministry in the temple. Now he sees a widow putting a few coins into the offering box. This seems unimpressive, but Jesus points out that the woman has given all she had. Unlike the offerings of the rich—which are showy but not really sacrificial—this is a truly extravagant gift. It shows that the Lord is her hope, security, and treasure.

OPTIONAL EXTRA

Create a playlist of songs which express devotion to Jesus and share it with the group. Or ask everyone to suggest their own favorite worship songs. Encourage the group to listen to the playlist as a way of helping them to reflect and respond to Jesus with devotion and love. (A few song suggestions to get you started: How Great Thou Art; In Christ Alone; Tis So Sweet; My Jesus I Love Thee.)

GUIDANCE FOR QUESTIONS

1. How do you tell if someone really loves God? This question is designed to make you examine your assumptions about what devotion to God really looks like. Encourage group members to be honest about what they think and perhaps to give examples of people they know who seem particularly devoted or committed in their faith. Don't worry about what the right or wrong answer is—just explore what people think.

2. Look at verse 17. Why has God given the people the temple? It should be a house of prayer for all the nations.

• **What have they made it into instead?** A "den of robbers."

3. So what does Jesus do (v 15-16)? He drives out those who are selling and buying and forbids people from carrying anything through the temple.

4. What's wrong with this? What do you think they should have been doing instead? They should have been genuinely repenting of their sin.

5. What kind of heart does Jesus want his people to have (v 22-25)? He wants them to have hearts full of faith (v 22-24) and forgiveness (v 25): hearts which genuinely pursue God.

• **Why is forgiving others so important (v 25)?** Forgiving others and being forgiven by God are inseparably linked. If we don't forgive others, we can't expect God to forgive us. Why? Because if we will not forgive, it calls into question whether or not we really believe the gospel. When the debt others owe us seems bigger than the debt we owed God, we have lost sight of the cross.

6. APPLY: What does this passage teach us about prayer? How can we honor God properly in the way we pray?
• Don't just go through the motions. Real prayer comes from a heart full of faith—it is about what comes from the inside, not about external rituals. Prayer needs to be an act of devotion, not just a discipline to master.
• Don't be afraid to ask God for things. God is powerful and can do anything we ask. (NOTE: Jesus' words in verse 23 are about "this mountain," not any old mountain. He is talking about the mountain the temple stands on. So he is talking about destroying the temple. In 9:42 Jesus said that anyone who causes a little one to stumble would be better thrown into the

sea. The temple system has caused people to stumble. So Jesus will cause it to be cast into the sea—metaphorically speaking. Jesus is not telling us to go around asking God to throw mountains into seas!)

- Forgive. When you come to pray, consider whether you have anything against anyone, and forgive them. This may not be easy! But it is vital.

EXPLORE MORE
Read Mark 11:27-33
What do the religious leaders ask Jesus first (v 27)? What do you think is their motivation for asking it? Who has authorized Jesus to do "these things" (a reference to his recent actions in the temple)? They think they themselves have heaven's authorization and they have not authorized Jesus to do what he is doing. So who has? This is a trap. What is Jesus supposed to say? *By my own authority*? They will jump all over that. Will he say that God himself sent him—something that in their eyes is blasphemy? They are looking for him to say something that will get him in trouble. **What counter-question does Jesus ask (v 30)? Why is this a trap (v 31-32)?** Jesus quizzes them about John the Baptist. Did his baptism come from heaven (i.e. was he sent by God) or from man (i.e. did he invent the idea himself)? If they say, "From heaven," Jesus is going to say, "Why didn't you believe him?" But if they say, "From man," then they are expressing an unpopular opinion, which they do not want to do because they fear the people.

7. In verses 28-31, what question does the scribe ask and how does Jesus answer it? The scribe asks an amazing question: "Which commandment is the most important of all?" The first part of Jesus' answer takes us to the oneness

of God (see Deuteronomy 6:4). God is exclusively and uniquely God. So, the greatest command is to love God more than we love anything else. Jesus also gives a second, complementary command: we should love our neighbor as ourselves (see Leviticus 19:18).

8. Why do you think obeying these commandments is better than making sacrifices (v 32-34)? You could go through all the motions in the sacrificial system without having love for God. But love for God is what empowers obedience to the other commands of God, including making sacrifices. Remember the context: Jesus has been speaking against what has been happening in the temple. We can see how Jesus' words relate to his turning of the tables that enabled Jews to participate in the sacrificial system. It is all a sham. People have been doing all these activities without love for God or love for others. They have missed the main thing.

9. Why will the scribes Jesus talks about in verses 38-40 be condemned? Their devotion is actually self-promotion. They show off their devotion to God with long prayers, but what they really want is not the approval of God, but the approval of man. They ravenously crave greetings, recognition, and places of honor. They enjoy being religious celebrities. Not only this, they are also predators who prey upon the vulnerable. Jesus says that they devour widows' houses. This probably means that they abused the generosity and hospitality of poor and vulnerable widows—eating them out of house and home. Jesus says that "they will receive the greater condemnation" (v 40). God sees right through their religious and self-righteous showmanship. God is also the defender of the vulnerable and he will come after anyone who dares to prey upon them.

10. Jesus previously stopped offerings from being made in the temple. So why does he approve of the widow's offering (v 41-44)? The widow's offering is a picture of true devotion. By giving "all she had to live on" and leaving herself to rely completely on the Lord, she showed that the Lord was her hope and trust and security and treasure, not financial security. She was not rich in finances, but rich in faith. The widow demonstrates that it is not the temple system itself that is corrupt—it's the people. It's good to offer sacrifices and offerings to God, but only if this is an expression of genuine devotion.

11. APPLY: Think about some sacrifices people might make for the Lord today. How can these be an expression of faith? People may give up time, money, or possessions for God. They may move to a different place to serve a particular community, deny themselves nice things in order to provide for others, or spend their leisure time on missions of mercy. All these are expressions of faith because they demonstrate that the Lord is our hope and security and priority, not material things or personal comfort.

- **But when do they become just formalities?** Jesus cares about what is inside our hearts, not external things. It's possible to keep on going through the motions of service and sacrifice while not having a heart of true faith and devotion. This might happen because you have lost sight of your need for Jesus. It could be a result of circumstances changing, so that what used to be a great sacrifice now isn't—for example, your salary goes up but you still give the same amount of money

away. You're no longer really depending on God, but outwardly you still look like you're doing the right thing.

12. APPLY: How can we guard our hearts against hypocrisy and truly devote ourselves to God?

- Recognize who God is. "He is one, and there is no other besides him" (Mark 12:32). He alone is worthy of every fiber of our devotion and affection and commitment. We can keep reminding ourselves of this by praising God for who he is.
- Focus on the cross. Jesus tells a story in Matthew 18:21-35 about a king who forgave his servant a debt. The servant then refused to forgive another man a much smaller debt. The king responded in anger! We need to keep in mind how much Jesus has done for us—that will motivate us not only to forgive others but to love them as ourselves.
- Be other-person-centered, not you-centered. Christian service is not just about signing up for enough church rotas—it's about genuinely concerning ourselves with others' needs, asking ourselves what we can do for them and how we can love them.
- Don't tell other people about the sacrifices you're making. Jesus draws a contrast between the showiness of the scribes and the hiddenness of the widow. Their devotion is a shiny counterfeit. Her devotion has a hidden genuineness to it. We should give and serve as an expression of praise, not as a strategy to get praise.

9 Mark 13:28 – 14:72
THE END DRAWS NEAR

THE BIG IDEA

Jesus planned his death, and it was agonizing for him. So don't take it for granted. We must stay alert—recognizing the amazing work of Jesus in his first coming, and living lives of readiness for his second coming.

SUMMARY

As Jesus' time in the temple comes to an end, he predicts its destruction (13:2). Then he continues to speak about the future (v 3-27). He seems to be talking about two timeframes at once: the destruction of the temple in AD 70, and the end of the age, when Jesus will come again. But Mark 13 is not only about the second coming. Jesus is also talking about events that are just about to take place.

Jesus warns his disciples to stay awake (v 28-37). They are like servants waiting for their master to return. The Lord is coming and they must be ready. Jesus highlights some explicit timeframes: evening, midnight, when the rooster crows, and in the morning.

In Mark 14:12-25, it is evening. Jesus and his disciples celebrate Passover. There are plots swirling around Jesus to kill him, but he walks through these events with a sovereign freedom and a striking note of authority. He predicts his betrayal (v 18-21) and explains his death and resurrection (v 22-25). He shows patience toward his disciples, who have failed to understand his repeated predictions of his death and resurrection.

Next it is midnight (v 26-42)—signaled by the singing of a hymn, which was usually done at midnight in the Passover traditions.

Jesus warns the disciples that they will abandon and even deny him (v 27-31). Yet the disciples are not awake, spiritually speaking. They think that nothing could ever destroy their commitment to him.

They go to Gethsemane, about half a mile from the city (v 32-42). Here Jesus prays three times, while urging the disciples three times to stay awake. Mark emphasizes Jesus' agony as he wrestles with and accepts the Father's will for his death. He is totally awake to the plan of his Father—while his disciples are literally fast asleep. They are not ready for Jesus' coming.

Next Judas arrives with soldiers and Jesus is arrested (v 43-52). Jesus is put on trial before the Jewish religious leaders (v 53-65). They, too, have not understood who he is—although their words, ironically, do reveal his identity. Jesus tells them that he is the Messiah and that they will see him coming on the clouds of heaven (v 62). They condemn him for blasphemy, and he is mocked and beaten.

Finally we see Peter in a trial of his own (v 66-72). The servant girl of the high priest recognizes him as one of Jesus' followers. Peter denies Jesus three times. Then the rooster crows—just as Jesus predicted. Peter breaks down and weeps. It is as though he has been asleep and his master has taken him by surprise.

OPTIONAL EXTRA

Act out the story Jesus tells in Mark 13:34-36. Start with a scene in which the master leaves, giving instructions to his servants; then have fun imagining what the servants might get up to instead; finally, finish with a scene in which the master returns and finds them asleep.

GUIDANCE FOR QUESTIONS

1. When you're about to see a loved one you haven't seen for a long time, what might you do to get ready? Answers might include tidying and cleaning, cooking a special meal, buying a present, dressing up nicely, or planning out all the things you're going to do together! This question introduces the theme of being ready or alert for Jesus' return.

2. Why have the disciples got to "stay awake" (v 32-37)? What does Jesus mean by this? They must "be on guard" (v 33). They should always be ready, because they (and even Jesus himself) do not know when the time will come. Jesus' example of servants waiting for their master suggests that what the disciples are waiting for is the coming of the Lord.

• What time periods does he mention (v 35)? In the evening, at midnight, when the rooster crows, and in the morning.

3. What moments in this passage show us that Jesus is in control of what is happening?

• v 12-16: Jesus sends his disciples to find a room to celebrate the Passover, predicting an encounter with a man carrying some water. Things happen exactly like Jesus said they would.

• v 18-20: Jesus reveals that he knows exactly who is going to betray him.

• v 21: he says that this betrayal was prophesied. All things will happen according to what Scripture says.

• v 22-25: Jesus predicts his death once again.

• v 27, 30: Jesus predicts the disciples' abandonment of him—even to the finest detail of the rooster crowing.

• v 28: Jesus predicts his resurrection.

• Why is that important? Mark doesn't want us to draw the conclusion that Jesus is out of his depth. There are plots swirling around him to kill him, and his disciples are going to betray and abandon him. But Jesus walks through these events with a sovereign freedom and a striking note of authority. He will lay down his life of his own accord (John 10:18)—and raise it up as well. Jesus will die as part of God's all-wise, predestined plan: he goes "as it is written" (Mark 14:21).

4. What do verses 22-25 reveal about why Jesus came?

• v 22-23: Jesus uses bread and wine to explain the divine design for his death in pictorial form. The broken bread represents his body and the wine represents the shedding of his blood. Jesus is going to die.

• v 24: The phrase "blood of the covenant" helps us understand why. The old covenant was established when Moses threw the blood of a sacrificial animal over the people as they promised to keep God's commandments (Exodus 24:3-8). The blood symbolized the sealing of the covenant. But the prophets announced that a day would come when God would make a new covenant with his people (Jeremiah 31:31-34). Jesus says that that day has now come. This new covenant is purchased and sealed with the lifeblood of the Lamb of God, slain for sinners. He died to save us and bring us to God.

• v 25: This verse hints at the fact that Jesus will rise again, and at the fact that he is bringing about the kingdom of God.

5. How do Peter and the other disciples demonstrate their lack of "alertness" in verses 27-31? How would you describe their response? They all swear that they will not fall away or deny Jesus. They take it for granted that they will never fall, instead of listening to his warnings. We might describe them as hasty, thoughtless, heedless, and even arrogant.

6. APPLY: Jesus' command to stay awake is for all of us (13:37). Now it is Jesus' second coming that we need to be ready for. We need to be spiritually awake. What do you think it looks like to be ready for Jesus' return? Look at the following verses to help you.
- **13:34:** Like the servants Jesus describes, we have been left with work to do. When Jesus returns, we want him to find us living the kind of life he has called us to: growing in love and knowledge of him, serving others, and seeking his will.
- **13:21-23 (if you have time):** We should not allow ourselves to be led astray by false teachers. Instead we should seek to grow in knowledge of Jesus so that we can recognize him when he comes.
- **14:27-31:** Unlike the disciples, we should be alert to the possibility of falling into sin.
- **14:37-38 (if you have time):** We should pray for God's help and protection against temptation.

7. How does Mark help us feel the agony of Jesus in these verses?
- Mark piles up words for emotional turmoil: Jesus is "greatly distressed and troubled" (v 33). Jesus himself describes himself as "very sorrowful" (v 34).
- When Jesus prays, he does not just get on his knees—he falls to the ground (v 35).
- The words of Jesus' prayer reveal his

agony. He wrestles with the divine will of the Father (v 36). The fact that he needed to pray multiple times shows how hard this prayer was.

8. How does he emphasize the failure of the disciples to stay awake? Jesus has to tell the disciples three times to watch and stay awake (v 34, 38, 41). Repeatedly, he finds them sleeping. Mark portrays the disciples as being in a total stupor—their eyes are heavy and they just can't stay awake, even though they have no excuse (v 40).

9. What moments in Jesus' trial (v 53-65) hint at who Jesus really is?
- v 55-56: the failure of the accusers to come up with coherent charges against Jesus reveals his innocence. This hints at his perfect sinlessness.
- v 58: Jesus really is building a new temple—a new way of coming to God.
- v 61: the high priest recognizes who Jesus is: "the Christ, the Son of the Blessed."
- **Yet how do we see the total rejection of Jesus as Lord here?**
  - 14:64: The high priest believes that Jesus is blaspheming. The irony is that he just committed blasphemy. The eternal God is standing before him, and he condemns him to death.
  - v 65: Jesus is mocked and beaten by the council members and guards.

10. What do Jesus' responses in verses 60-62 tell us about him?
- First, Jesus is silent. This shows his willingness to go to his death: he doesn't try to defend himself or argue with his accusers. It is a fulfillment of Isaiah 53:7, part of a passage which describes a promised Suffering Servant who would die for the sins of the world. So this detail also reveals Jesus' identity as the Messiah.

- Then Jesus makes his claim clear. Is he the Christ? "I am," he says (Mark 14:62). The title "Son of Man," the right hand of Power, and the clouds of heaven are all references to Daniel 7:13-14, a prophecy about the Messiah (see EXPLORE MORE below).
- Jesus' promise in Mark 14:62 also reveals that he is already looking forward to his resurrection and return. He knows that his crucifixion will not be the end of the story.

EXPLORE MORE
Read Daniel 7:13-14
What is given to the Son of Man? Dominion (authority to rule) and glory and a kingdom—incorporating all peoples and nations.
What is his future? His reign will last forever.
How might this change the way we look at our own future? Jesus' rule will never be destroyed. So we can put ourselves in his hands knowing that nothing can take us away from him. We can entrust our future to him—just as, in the garden and in the trial, Jesus entrusted his own future to his Father.

11. Why does Peter deny Jesus (14:66-72)? What do you think is going through his mind throughout this scene? Peter is presumably afraid of what will happen to him if he acknowledges the fact that he knows Jesus. But the heart of the matter is that he is not spiritually awake. Peter has never fully understood Jesus and his mission—he has been thinking the things of man, not the things of God (see 8:33). Finally, when the rooster crows, Peter realizes his mistake—and weeps. It is as though he has been asleep and his master has taken him by surprise.

12. APPLY: We have all failed Jesus, denied him, and rejected him at different times. But why does Mark 14 offer us hope?
- Jesus was perfectly innocent, yet he willingly went to his death for sinners. Peter's agony in verse 72 as he realizes his sin is nothing compared to Jesus' agony in Gethsemane. If we feel agonized about our sin, we can know that Jesus suffered far greater agony in order to make us guiltless before God.
- The lead-up to the crucifixion shows us Jesus' patient attitude toward his disciples. They are spiritually blind and slow to understand what he has already told them about his coming death and resurrection—yet he explains it again in the Last Supper (v 22-24). He knows they will betray, deny, and abandon him—yet he shares a meal with them. They fail to stay awake—yet he keeps giving them more chances (v 32-41). If this is Jesus' attitude toward his disciples, it is also his attitude toward us. We can trust him to be patient and kind to us even when we fail.

Mark 15:16 – 16:8
THE DIVINE KING

THE BIG IDEA

Jesus was utterly forsaken to bring us near to God. His death and resurrection reveal him as the true King of the world. He has saved us—so let's respond with awe and hope.

SUMMARY

Mark 15 highlights how Jesus is utterly forsaken at the cross. There is rejection at the surface, but there is something much deeper happening beneath the surface. Mark keeps highlighting this dissonance.

After a trial before Pilate (v 1-15) Jesus is taken away by Roman soldiers, who take special pains to mock him to the maximum degree (v 16-20). The irony is unmistakeable. The purple robe, the crown of thorns, the chanting and acclaiming as "King of the Jews," the reed, the kneeling and bowing—it all bears royal connotations. The reader recognizes the truth hidden behind the soldiers' scorn: Jesus is royalty.

Verses 21-27 set the stage for the drama of the crucifixion. Mark draws our attention to details which show the pain Jesus was in and the shame that was inflicted upon him. He then takes us through a series of concentric circles of rejection, moving closer to the cross. First we stand on the outskirts and see people passing by, who mock Jesus from a distance (v 29-30). Drawing nearer, we see the religious leaders (v 31-32). Again these people say more than they know. They say, "He saved others; he cannot save himself." The truth is that he cannot save others and himself. He can only save others by staying on the cross. Finally, those on the other two crosses join in the mockery (v 32).

The center is the cross (v 33-37). The scene changes as an unnatural darkness descends. In this climactic moment, the Father placed the sin of the world upon his Son. Jesus experienced the searing pain of separation from God and the damnation of God. He cries, "Why have you forsaken me?" This comes from Psalm 22. This psalm opens with the question of why God has forsaken the Messiah. But it ends with the answer: so that the nations can come to God in worship. The answer to Jesus' question is: so that sinners could be accepted. Jesus was forsaken so that those who are in him would never be. This is why the temple curtain, which represented the separation between God and people, is torn in two (v 38). Access to God is now available.

Straight away we see a right response to the cross. The Roman centurion watches Jesus die with a loud shout of victory and responds with a confession of faith (v 39).

Mark introduces the women who stood looking on (v 40-41). This functions as a bridge to the next section. It is now Friday evening (v 42-47) and there is a rush to bury Jesus before the Sabbath day starts. Joseph of Arimathea—an unlikely follower of Jesus, as a member of the ruling council—requests Jesus' body. Pilate, surprised that Jesus is already dead, grants his request. Jesus is buried in the tomb of a rich man—as Isaiah 53:9 predicted.

Mark 16 opens with three women who go to the tomb (v 1-3). They expect to see his body and anoint it with spices that would offset the odor that would come from decomposition. But when they arrive, they find that the stone has been rolled away (v 4)! The tomb is empty. They meet a messenger from heaven who explains why: Jesus has risen (v 5-7).

The women are filled with fear because their expectations have been completely overturned (v 8)—and the Gospel of Mark comes to an end. It is fitting that Mark closes his Gospel with fear. He is reminding us that Jesus is far greater than what we expect or imagine. He is both awesome and terrifying!

OPTIONAL EXTRA

Watch a clip online from a movie version of Jesus' life, showing the crucifixion. (For example, there are clips from the 2000 film *The Miracle Maker* readily available.) Not all the details will be exactly the same as in Mark's Gospel, but it may help you to visualize and connect emotionally with the scene.

GUIDANCE FOR QUESTIONS

1. Why do you think it can hurt so much to be rejected or abandoned by others? This question is a way of helping the group to start feeling the emotion of the cross, as Jesus is utterly forsaken. It hurts to be rejected because we are made for relationship with one another! You may like to encourage group members to share stories of when they felt abandoned, if they feel comfortable doing so. Or if it's easier, keep the conversation more abstract.

2. How does the soldiers' mockery of Jesus actually reveal who he really is (v 16-20)? The purple robe, the crown of thorns, the chanting and acclaiming as "King of the Jews," the reed, the kneeling and bowing—it all bears royal connotations. The soldiers are mocking Jesus, but there is truth hidden behind the scorn. He is royalty:

he should be dressed in royal robes with a crown and a reed. They should anoint him, hail him as King, and bow before him. The truth of Jesus' deity is suppressed, but at the same time they almost can't help expressing it, even in a twisted and perverted way.

3. In verses 21-27, what do we find out about how Jesus is treated?
- Simon had to carry Jesus' cross for him (v 21). This bears testimony to the gory truth that Jesus had been beaten so mercilessly that he was unable to carry his own crossbeam.
- Sour wine mixed with myrrh (v 23) was a narcotic, so its purpose was to deaden the pain—pointing to the agony that Jesus was in. But it was probably also part of the mockery, since a cup of wine would normally be offered to a victorious king.
- The soldiers divide up Jesus' clothing (v 24). He has lost everything he has. He has been shamed to the full extent that the soldiers can achieve.
- He is crucified alongside two robbers (v 27)—being "numbered with the transgressors," as Isaiah 53:12 predicted.

4. Who else is Jesus rejected and mocked by (v 29-32)? Passers by (v 29), the chief priests and scribes (v 31-32), and the two criminals being crucified with Jesus (v 32).

- **Jesus is King. If that's so, what should he do, according to these mockers?** He should save himself (v 30, 32).

5. Where does the climax of Jesus' suffering and rejection by others come? In verses 33-34. The Father, who has eyes too pure to behold sin, turns his face away from his Son for the first and only time. Jesus endures a moment of separation from God. This is shown by his cry in verse 34 and by the unnatural darkness, a sign of God's judgment (see Amos 8:9-10).

6. What happened as Jesus breathed his last (v 37-39)? The temple curtain was torn in two. A Roman centurion recognized Jesus' true identity as the Son of God.

• **What do you think made the centurion realize who Jesus was?** The centurion saw the way Jesus breathed his last (v 39). He saw that Jesus died with a "loud cry" (v 37): a shout of victory, not a whimper of defeat. Then God opened his eyes to understand who Jesus really is.

7. APPLY: How does it feel to know that Jesus was forsaken by his Father so that you could be accepted? One-word answers are fine! Encourage the group to marvel at the cross and to take the opportunity to reflect more deeply on the wonders of salvation.

• **What are some ways in which you can put into practice Psalm 22's call to worship Jesus, serve him, and proclaim that "he has done it"?** Try to be practical here, so that everyone has one action point to go away with. You might discuss singing or bowing down or other forms of physical worship. You might talk about ways to devote your lives more fully to Jesus. You could discuss friends or family members with who you could share the good news, or talk about good ways to teach it to children.

EXPLORE MORE
Read Mark 15:40-47
Why is Joseph of Arimathea a surprising disciple of Jesus (v 43)? He is a respected member of the Jewish ruling council, which condemned Jesus.
Why is Pilate surprised (v 44)? Jesus is

already dead.
Jesus died as a convicted criminal, but how is he buried? He is buried like a rich man. This matters because it is a fulfillment of Isaiah 53:9: "They made his grave with the wicked and with a rich man in his death."

8. What are the women expecting when they go to the tomb (16:1-3)? They think Jesus' body will be starting to decay, so they are going to anoint him with spices. They expect to see and to care for a corpse. They also expect to have trouble rolling away the heavy stone at the entrance to the tomb.

9. What do they discover instead (v 4-6)? The tomb is empty and the stone has been rolled away! They meet a messenger from heaven who explains why: Jesus has risen.

10. Why do you think they are so afraid (v 8)? Their expectations have been completely overturned. The gospel of Jesus Christ shatters all our categories and leaves us with shock and awe!

11. The Gospel of Mark ends very abruptly. How does that affect our final impression of Jesus? It is fitting that Mark closes his Gospel with fear. He is reminding us that Jesus is far greater than what we expect or imagine. He is both awesome and terrifying! This abrupt ending leaves us with a lasting impression of the shock of the resurrection—capturing how amazing this one-off event was.

12. APPLY: In what ways does the resurrection of Jesus change our perspective on life here and now? So many people today live in despair and darkness. They don't know about the bright victory of Easter Sunday. But as followers of Jesus we look at the empty tomb in stunned silence, shock, and awe. And the resurrection allows us to know hope even in dark times. Jesus has won. He has defeated death. That hope can't fail or die.

- **What will you do and say in response?** Perhaps you will speak words of hope into situations of darkness. Perhaps you will stop fearing difficulties here on earth because you know that they will come to an end. Perhaps you will give yourself more to God's work on earth now, because you know that God's kingdom is what we hope in, the one thing that will not fade away. This might include giving money, speaking about Jesus to unbelievers, or any number of other things.

Dive deeper into Mark's Gospel

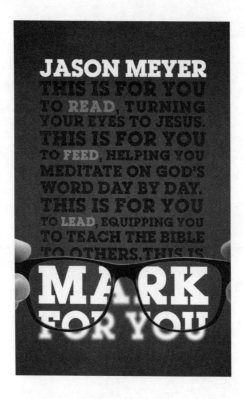

"If I have a first love in Scripture, it is Mark's Gospel and the Jesus who stands forth from its pages."

Join Jason Meyer as he unpacks Mark verse by verse, helping you to turn your eyes to Jesus—his power, his wisdom, and his compassionate heart. This accessible and absorbing expository guide can be used for personal devotions, alongside small-group studies, or for sermon preparation.

Good Book Guides
The full range

2 Corinthians 8–13:
7 Studies
James Hughes

Galatians: 7 Studies
Timothy Keller

Ephesians: 10 Studies
Thabiti Anyabwile

Ephesians: 8 Studies
Richard Coekin

Philippians: 7 Studies
Steven J. Lawson

Colossians: 6 Studies
Mark Meynell

1 Thessalonians: 7 Studies
Mark Wallace

1&2 Timothy: 7 Studies
Phillip Jensen

Titus: 5 Studies
Tim Chester

Hebrews: 8 studies
Michael J. Kruger

Hebrews: 8 Studies
Justin Buzzard

James: 6 Studies
Sam Allberry

1 Peter: 6 Studies
Juan R. Sanchez

2 Peter & Jude: 6 Studies
Miguel Núñez

1 John: 7 Studies
Nathan Buttery

Revelation: 7 Studies
Tim Chester

TOPICAL

Man of God: 10 Studies
Anthony Bewes & Sam Allberry

Biblical Womanhood:
10 Studies
Sarah Collins

The Apostles' Creed:
10 Studies
Tim Chester

The Lord's Prayer:
7 Studies
Tim Chester

Promises Kept: Bible Overview: 9 Studies
Carl Laferton

The Reformation Solas
6 Studies
Jason Helopoulos

Contentment: 6 Studies
Anne Woodcock

Women of Faith:
8 Studies
Mary Davis

Meeting Jesus: 8 Studies
Jenna Kavonic

Heaven: 6 Studies
Andy Telfer

Mission: 7 Studies
Alan Purser

Making Work Work:
8 Studies
Marcus Nodder

The Holy Spirit: 8 Studies
Pete & Anne Woodcock

Experiencing God:
6 Studies
Tim Chester

Real Prayer: 7 Studies
Anne Woodcock

Church: 8 Studies
Anne Woodcock

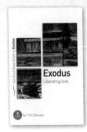
Exodus
Liberating love

Romans 8–16
In view of God's mercy

Real Prayer
Connecting with our heavenly Father

God's Word For You

Galatians For You

"The book of Galatians is dynamite. It is an explosion of joy and freedom which leaves us enjoying a life of blessing. I pray that it explodes in your heart as you read this book."

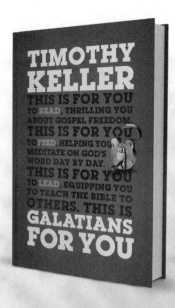

Daniel For You

"The book of Daniel offers you the knowledge that God is still at work, the confidence that it is possible to remain faithful to Jesus Christ, and the strength to live for him in our day."

Find out more about these resources at:

www.thegoodbook.com/for-you

The Whole Series

Join the *explore* community

The *Explore* Facebook group is a community of people who use *Explore* to study the Bible each day.

This is the place to share your thoughts, questions, encouragements, and prayers as you read *Explore*, and interact with other readers, as well as contributors, from around the world. No questions are too simple or too difficult to ask.

JOIN NOW:
facebook.com/groups/tgbc.explore

BIBLICAL | RELEVANT | ACCESSIBLE

At The Good Book Company, we are dedicated to helping Christians and local churches grow. We believe that God's growth process always starts with hearing clearly what he has said to us through his timeless word—the Bible.

Ever since we opened our doors in 1991, we have been striving to produce Bible-based resources that bring glory to God. We have grown to become an international provider of user-friendly resources to the Christian community, with believers of all backgrounds and denominations using our books, Bible studies, devotionals, evangelistic resources, and DVD-based courses.

We want to equip ordinary Christians to live for Christ day by day, and churches to grow in their knowledge of God, their love for one another, and the effectiveness of their outreach.

Call us for a discussion of your needs or visit one of our local websites for more information on the resources and services we provide.

Your friends at The Good Book Company

thegoodbook.com | thegoodbook.co.uk
thegoodbook.com.au | thegoodbook.co.nz
thegoodbook.co.in